LIFE IN A PAPER BAG

LIFE IN A PAPER BAG

JILLIAN RICHARDS

EPIGRAPH BOOKS
RHINEBECK, NEW YORK

Life in a Paper Bag © 2020 by Jillian Richards

Paperback ISBN 978-1-951937-63-8
eBook ISBN 978-1-951937-64-5

Library of Congress Control Number 2020919617

Book design by Colin Rolfe

Epigraph Books
22 East Market Street, Suite 304
Rhinebeck, NY 12572
(845) 876-4861
epigraphps.com

A man needs a little madness ...
or else he never cuts the rope to be free.

—ZORBA THE GREEK

REGARD

I regard my life.
I regard the manner
in which I have been gifted.

I regard
that which has been withheld.

I regard moments,
rare moments
of pure joy.

I regard love,
and the clarity of guilessness.

I regard
moments in my life
frozen in time.

Moments
of disbelief
and of surprise,

of wisdom
and of helplessness,
of terror
and of wonder,
of astonishment
and of anguish.

Moments of embarrassment
and of pain.

Moments of insensitivity
and moments of revelation,
and
moments of grace.

SOMEBODY

Each morning for six weeks I crossed the lobby of the
DoubleTree Hilton Hotel. As I was scurrying across the tiles on
my way to an early morning appointment, a young man who
worked in the hotel approached me. "Excuse me," he apologized.
"I've been watching you for a few weeks. Are you *somebody*?"

I took a deep breath in order not to embarrass him with
my mirth, raised my nose an inch, and made his day by saying
yes in a firm voice—as much as to say, "How could you even
need to ask?" As I continued on across the lobby, I could see
him with his colleagues, laughing and pointing. "I told you!" I
heard him say.

There were a lot of *somebodies* in the USA, or a lot of folk who were damned sure that they were *somebody*. One craggy-faced gentleman I met at a Hollywood "do" was utterly miffed when I offered my hand and said, "Good evening. My name is Jillian. I am sorry—I do not know your name." *He* sure did, and was not about to tell me. How dare I not know that he was *somebody*.

Time after time, as I was standing in an airport or other public place I would be approached by an excited and persistent person who usually started with—*I know you.* "I don't think so," I would demur. It took me weeks to realize that this only led to more and more determination. "I do! I've seen you in the movies!" "Sorry, no." "Oh no, sorry. I've seen you on television." "No, you must have mistaken me for someone else." These conversations went on for five or six minutes before I was able to extricate myself with grace.

I began to expect such accostings and prepared a response that got me off the hook by replying, "Thank you!" while flashing my most brilliant Australian smile as I walked away. That was all they needed. They knew they were right. Who was I to dissuade them?

But I did have the privilege of meeting quite a few real somebodies, gracious and charming—and other. When I met Larry King, I was wearing my favorite black-and-white striped suit. "What's with the striped suit?" he asked.

What was a girl to say? "I like it," I said, somewhat defensive. I wish I had been quick enough to ask him to sign across it with a big black marking pen. I will be quicker if I meet him again.

At a large gathering in Hollywood, wreathed in that black and white striped suit that never did get Larry King's signature, I was asked to sit down with a couple I had not previously met.

The lady was curious about me. Who was I? Why had we not met before? Where was I from? Where did I purchase my outfit? Unused to such interrogation, I made inquiries about her later, to discover that she was the well-known Abigail Van Buren of the "Dear Abbey" advice column. At one time more than twelve hundred newspapers ran her column.

Bedecked in a sparkly creation, I went off to Hollywood for another black-tie event. The young people who escorted us to our seats each had perfect teeth, perfect hair, perfect skin, perfect bodies, and perfect manners. The handsome young man who escorted me to my chair chatted away and then said, "I remember you, but I am sorry—I do not remember you name. Would you mind if I had my photograph taken with you?" I would not. Once more, I felt like a stranger in a strange land, Hollywood Land, unseen for who I was, but seen for who I might be.

Wreathed in black-and-white stripes.

Who might I be?

Classy in black

In that same DoubleTree Hilton, I settled on a favorite breakfast of coffee, wheat toast, and fresh Hawaiian pineapple. One particularly busy morning at work, the phone rang with an urgent request for me to contact a high-profile guest who was staying in the same hotel. "Sure, I will be back to you in a moment." But across the way at the DoubleTree Hilton the girl at the switchboard was in no way going to reveal that they had any such guest walking their hallowed halls. I asked for the supervisor, but no, still no acknowledgment of said guest. Time was short and I had pulled out all the stops I could think of, while understanding the hotel's need to be discreet. Who did I know in the hotel who may be able to bypass protocol without causing trouble?

A flash of inspiration led me to call the restaurant and ask for my waiter by name. "Hi!" I said. "This is Jillian. Do you remember me?"

"Oh, yes," he laughed, "wheat toast and pineapple!" I guess I have to be famous for something.

Draping around the world in yellow.

TRYING TO BREATHE—TRYING TO THINK

During so many moments in my life I have stood deathly still, stunned and shocked as events have left me emotionally naked and totally unarmed. It has been with a cry for grace that I have learned to breathe again through the veil of incredulity to resilience, as I have paused my thinking and searched for wisdom, courage, hope, and laughter. I have searched for a breath of truth to cleanse my spirit. There have been so many surprises. Some have offered me joy, some have been injurious to my body, and some have wounded my spirit so deeply that it has taken all my courage to begin to live again. As my boys grew and entered their adulthood years, I pontificated lovingly that, "I do not know what life will bring to you. The only thing I can promise you is surprises." Having learned most of that which I treasure by the bumps and jerks and calamities of my life, it was as simple and clear an offering as I could bring to them. But I did not have to preach it to them, and I am sorry if I pontificated.

Through my infancy, childhood and teenage years I was trained to conform. I should not think, and I should look as though I was venerating whichever adult male was offering a point of view. Nothing was to be questioned. *Should* and *ought* were featured.

Our religious group of "Featheries" has been so named by some who have kept up a loving friendship over the years, aware that we are birds of a feather. Who else could understand that we were a religious group secluded from the world? There were embarrassing evenings when an adult male was moved to travel into Melbourne town with the express purpose of standing in the vicinity of Young and Jackson's pub yelling at all "the rabble" who passed by that they had jolly-well-better be careful, or they might be doomed to eternal damnation. The person moved to berate the passing crowds was always a man.

Women were supposed to be silent and submit. And wear hats. They were not to wear pants or makeup for fear of being condemned and considered to be *like Jezebel.* No matter how mortified or embarrassed I felt, *I had no right to speak up.* None of us was allowed to dance, go to the movies, make too much noise, or have close friendships with Roman Catholic neighbors. None of us was allowed to play outside on Sundays or question things we did not understand. Thinking of it, it makes me feel as though none of us was allowed to breathe. It was and is, a long and often-confusing path learning to be fully alive.

And then, on one bright day I went to live in Chicago. In that cultured and cultivated city of music and architecture, art and lake—I worked for a wonderful period with a group of the Sisters of Charity. The first of these sisters whom I met almost bowled me over with her energy and glowing beauty. She was a superstar named Sister Phillip. Within the fold of the little Roman Catholic church where we all worked, endeavoring to offer language, hope, and a modicum of freedom to the tiny hearing-impaired bairns who were placed into our charge, I learned that the Featheries were not the only encumbered religious group. The walls of religiosity began to crumble. It was as if the Lord was saying to me, "Look and see. You were not the only one imprisoned. You are not different. You and these black-garbed sisters are the same. You are one."

It was there that I listened with reverent wonder as a sister told me that she had joined the order so that she could help the community. But at 7:00 p.m. each evening the gates to her convent were closed. She was locked in. And the world she wanted to serve was locked out. She was sad as she said this, wistful and longing. She was considering leaving the order. It was in that holy place of learning that I had the effrontery to ask one of the lovely mothers what was the *real* name of her son, Fats. "Fats," she said. And I died.

DAMAGED GOODS

I met a man
in the elevator today.
"Where are you going?"
I asked.
"To the third floor,"
  he said.
"So am I,"
I said.
I pressed the button,
and up we went.
He was wheeling
a heavy-looking suitcase.
"That looks serious,"
  I said.
"It is,"
he said.
"May I ask what is in it?"
"Oh yes,"
he said,

"it is meditation tapes."
"Who is meditating?"
I asked.
"Oh,
it's just the bible,"
he said.
"Oh,"
I said.
"Here,"
he said,
"let me give you one.
I have a damaged one
I don't mind giving up."

I didn't want
a damaged one.

But the paper bag of life can bring dreadful damage.

ON A PHOTOGRAPH

Auntie Dell hovered through life in a cloud of perfume and furs, always wearing a huge wobbling bunch of purple silk violets on her lapel. Named Adele Capuano, she was fourteen years older than my mother, Annie Merle. Sensual and attractive even in her later years, she was bespoke femininity. No trousers for Auntie Dell. No masculine shirts. No flat shoes. She overflowed with graceful ease and loving care. Apart from

Youthful Auntie Dell in 1919.

the fact that she told me once that a woman should never consider showing her arms after a certain age, I do not remember her sharing intimate thoughts with me. But I did know that she loved me.

It was Merle, the youngest of my many siblings, who told me about Bill. I do not remember where we were when she told me, and I do not remember how old I was, but I do remember a deathly silence rushing to enclose the words. I remember my feeling of fear should I inadvertently let out a whimper of the story in front of Auntie Dell.

I treasure the one photograph I have of Bill as a young man. He was tall, fair-haired, blue-eyed, and handsome. Sitting proudly beside him is his brown-haired, brown-eyed sparrow of a fiancée who lived in Tasmania, a foreign land to me. I did not meet her either. Bill is wearing his Air Force pilot's uniform. The year was 1940.

Bill was shot down and killed on his first mission over Greece during World War II. Auntie Dell grieved silently. Palpably. And we could not speak about it. Pilot Officer William Leslie Topp died on February 28, 1944. He is buried in the British War Cemetery in Athens.

William Leslie Topp with his fiancée.

SPLIT

As I stepped into her kitchen, she turned away from me to stare into the opaque glass of her oven door. I was fused to the heat of her pain. She twisted her body and looked at my shoes, her breathing awkward. Speech attempted to clamber up from inside her. "I get awkward stares from strangers," was her greeting to me. "That's what I'm hiding from in here," pointing at her oven in agonized desperation. "Even my closest friends move away from me," she anguished. "I know they are trying to come towards me, but all their movements jerk them away. They are alarmed or something, maybe agitated. So am I," she whispered to herself, "so am I," her arms hugging her chest.

She told me of friends whose self-aware anxiety led to a quick downward sweeping of their eyes and a blind patting of her hand, which made her feel as though she was banished.

She was trying to see me but could not see past her heart, so occupied was she with her pain. I had been invited to meet her by a friend who believed I might understand. "They told me that I would get over it," she anguished, her breath strangled with pain. "I should be over it!" she howled, bent over herself. "It's nine months now. I should be over it!"

A morning outing with her son had started so happily. Nine years old and full of the joys of childhood, he had romped on ahead of her like an eager bear cub emerging from winter hibernation, awake to the wonders of his own world of nine-year-old bliss. The traffic lights turned to green, and as the gaggle of pedestrians moved to cross the road, her son ran on ahead looking for adventures on the other side of the road.

And time split. A young driver, cursed now with guilt for the rest of his life, mistook his timing, missed the red light, and took the life of her son. In an instant. In front of her.

And someone told her she that she should be over it? How could they?

I was put to thinking deeply about platitudes as I left. Is it possible that hidden inside a well-meant attempt to bring freedom can lurk confusion? This beautiful young woman would not "get over it." What should she say when she was asked if she had children, and then how many? Should she say that she had two, and then try to explain? Or should she say that she had one, and then try to explain? Her life was changed forever. She would be different forever. From one blessed moment to one cursed moment, she was hurled unbidden into the world of women who have lost a beloved child.

Incomplete thought can be thoughtless or even unintentionally hurtful. It is always confusing. It is possible to be patronizing even when well intentioned. Quick words with the offer of quick fixes can become platitudes. If we hurt as did this young woman, we present challenge and even offense. If only our lives would go right back to the way they were, to a more comfortable place, "they" could feel in control of their own lives once more and be at peace—if only we would let them.

It takes guts to stand close to someone who is stuck, bringing our own self, humbled by our inability to fix.

We offer ourselves.
We offer not platitudes.
We offer a cup of tea,
a tissue,
a cup of cold water
in the name of love.

O SYRIA, SYRIA

Peter Kujawinski was an American diplomat living in Israel in the year 2000 when he took time out to travel across Syria for a week, "after some nimble arranging." In his January 30, 2017 article for the New York Times, he wrote that the Middle East had been a more hopeful place seventeen years before.

Seventeen years before, I had been invited to visit both Israel and Syria, and I resisted because I was wearied from too much travel. I resisted also because I was still in protracted recovery following major surgery. But most of all, I resisted because I believed that the expense was not warranted. I punished the inviter mentally. He had an experienced minder, and I believed he would manage with distinction and without my assistance. My possible travel and accommodation were hard to justify on the one hand, yet exciting and hardly resistible on the other. From the safe distance offered by time, I am not convinced I made the correct decision. I did not go.

I had an elementary knowledge of the history of Israel, having imbibed details from friends who had traveled in and out of there more than eighty times, and who were in the end honored with an avenue of trees for their contributions. I had read many stories of bold Zionists, heroes, and heroines—including the statesman David Ben-Gurion and Golda Meir, Israel's fourth prime minister and own imperious iron lady. I had in my library a book entitled, *The Amazing Jew*. I was awed and fascinated by both the people and the land. But I had only a paltry knowledge of Syria's history and peoples. And I did not go.

A few months later I read about Aleppo for the first time, and I was mesmerized. I gathered to my bosom any article I could find on Aleppo. As I built my file, I was drawn to the city and to its history. I was going—and as soon as I could. But I did not go.

The hopefulness in the Middle East was blasted as it continues to be blasted, and I could not go. The file I still keep on Aleppo now seems like the wraith of a dead child. I weep, and have wept for Syria for years now. I weep for Aleppo and its generations of stories—ancient and lost. I weep for the people. I weep for their lack of green grass to walk on and their lack of fresh water to drink. I weep for a civilization punished just for existing. Even if I could go to Syria, I could not bear to see Aleppo. And I am sorry. The proud civilization it took centuries to build has taken such a painfully short time to destroy.

I beg the parents of my grandchildren to allow them to travel where they will. Let the teachings of the world break down their immature prejudices and open their hearts to the new and the different—to wonder and to awe.

I did not go to Syria. I did not see Aleppo. I could have. And I did not.

ON THE FLOOR

Most who sat watching the first moon landing on their television sets did not know that a windstorm in Australia almost interrupted that broadcast. At the Parkes Observatory in Australia, radio telescope operators worked desperately to receive the live video of Buzz Aldrin and Neil Armstrong stepping onto the pale, faraway orb of our moon. As the telescope operators were completing their gigantic part in this momentous event, howling winds kicked up.

In Salem, Massachusetts, darkness fell. Quiet reigned in front of millions of television sets worldwide while, at that historic moment in Salem, a young woman struggled with the horror of early pregnancy nausea and weariness from having behaved herself far too well for far too long. I was that young woman, too stupid to know that I was not up for entertaining, and too eager to watch the moon landing to put myself to bed. The visitors in my home had been fed and were settled down. Across the road, the Salem Witch House stared into the moonlight, not much impressed with the goings on up there in the heavens. It had seen enough of its own. And I was sinking closer and closer to the floor with every wave of nausea. The Parkes transmitter in Australia had a power output of 20 watts, and I had about the same power output in my living room.

Buzz and Neil had decided to skip their scheduled rest break and exit the spacecraft earlier than anticipated, with the result that the technicians in faraway Parkes needed to tilt their telescope towards the horizon. This had not been planned, and it was not easy.

In Salem, I needed to go to bed. This had not been planned either, but I was sinking. In Parkes, winds were kicking up, howling and complicating life, causing technical problems. Buffeting, shuddering and swaying occurred. The Australian movie, *The Dish*, demonstrates the buffeting winds in Parkes. Nothing demonstrates my sinking in Salem. Technicians fiddled in Parkes, and adjustments to a small toggle switch ultimately helped millions around the world to watch the moon landing right side up, instead of upside down, as had been threatened by the buffeting winds. But me? I did not see the landing. I succumbed to the desperate need to sleep on the floor in front of the television, in front of the iconic images transmitted with the help of some cunning Aussies. While I was sinking with the fading hope that I could remain awake long enough to see this world-shaking event, in Australia the winds rattled and shook and demanded attention, technicians rattled and shook in anxiety but persevered long enough to resolve the problem and begin to breathe again. I began to breathe again too. Gently and quietly, on the floor unnoticed by my guests. They loved the whole show and were effusive in their thanks as they left.

Around the world multitudes of viewers loved the whole show too and were effusive in their gratitude. Only a select few knew of the dramas with a toggle switch in Parkes that denied us all the need to stand on our heads to watch the first moon landing. And only I knew of the drama in Salem, where I had slept through the unfolding drama. It was riveting for millions, and an exhausting relief for the Australian technicians and their US counterparts. It was more than disappointing for me, although I am pleased that I did meet Buzz Aldrin some years later, and that he signed a photograph for me. I have it still. It stands alongside my deep disappointment at missing the show.

MOMENTS OF GRACE

I stood transfixed with wonder, bound to a new creation. Fresh as the breath of God, a babe had been born to me. I was ravished by my love for him and compelled towards him by feelings that so overwhelmed me I could hardly contain them. Life divided into before and after the day marked forever in the calendar of my life. I was his and he was mine, and I would keep him safe.

But not all was endless bliss. Life divided again one September morning. Our pediatrician came perilously close to bowling me over as he ran down the steps at the front of the Children's Hospital in Rhode Island. He stopped a moment, glancing at his watch. "I was going to call you. Nathan had a heart attack last night. He is intensive care." Then with another glance at his watch, "I am on a radio program in a few minutes. Have to run. Bye."

Nathan was nine months old. I was staggered, stunned, and desperate. I thought my heart would burst. I had left Nathan there as a failure-to-thrive baby. I could not breathe. I could not cry. But I could run. In intensive care I was not allowed to touch him. He was taped and tubed into an oxygen cocoon. I could only talk to him, compelling him to know my love. I was full to bursting with anguish.

On that hallowed ground between life and death I trod away the gentle hours, days, weeks, months and ultimately years.

He returned to us, thin, pale, and with a more tentative hold on life than I comprehended. As he grew, months of joy passed as his beloved brother Luke Benjamin was embraced into our family. Early mornings were filled with cries of, "Doll, doll, doll!" as Nathan pulled every stuffed toy down from the shelf and into Luke's cot where the two of them bounced around in glee. They became inseparable, grace upon grace, enhanced by such gems as Nathan holding aloft his latest art piece crying,

"See my half-part-sic-bun-wheel!" Nathan chattered and led while Luke chattered and followed. Luke bestowed us with such gifts as, "I love you behind my knees, Mummy."

Friend Ruth who had birthed five beautiful daughters decided that my boys needed a few of their girl toys to round out their development. Excitement reigned in our household as we waited for her arrival. She produced a doll, a bag full of doll clothes and a large plastic cot. Nathan loved the cot on sight, climbed into it, and smashed it to pieces.

Then, before I could say Jack Robinson, I was pregnant again. It was all as easy as shelling peas. Well, almost.

On one of his "at home and quite well days" Nathan and Luke and I visited a local shopping mall. I was fat and waddly, great with my third child. Neither Nathan nor Luke noticed that. They loved it all. A photo booth set up in the middle of the mall enticed us, so I slicked down their hair and propped them up for some super shots. Three days later we returned to make our selection. We were excited and even more excited when we found a large photo of Nathan had been placed in a prominent display position. Nathan was thrilled, and Luke was too young and sweet-natured to be jealous. "There I am, smiling at the world!" Nathan beamed, delighted that he was famous. Four days later Nathan died. And life divided again. I needed new words. I had become part of a new group, mothers who had lost their babies.

Four months later Toby John was born slap bang right into our hearts. Toby: "God is good." John: "graced by God." And such he became.

Time passed, and slowly, I learned the meaning of release. I learned to ponder Nathan's life silently. I learned that the shower is a good place to cry. I learned the deep value of friends who could help to bear the burden, laugh and cry with me, unafraid of my pain. Beloved friend Milt came to visit, and, as he cuddled Toby, he turned to me and whispered, "Do you believe in reincarnation?" They were like prints of each other.

I remember him, "smiling at the world."

Blessed memories.

OVER THAT BLOODY BRIDGE

His face dripping with sweat and his teeth flashing, "Ne me quitte pas," sang Jacques Brel. "*Ne me quitte pas.*" "If you go away. Please don't go away." Neil Diamond sang it too. And Barbra Streisand. And Terry Jacks. And others.

But they do go away. Over that bloody bridge. To a place where we can no longer reach them, even with a heart bursting with love. "Ne me quitte pas." "Please don't leave me." I listen, and I am wrenched with a spasm of longing and grief. "If you go away. Please don't go away."

Back and forth I walked. Barefoot. In slippers. In heels. In the night. In the day. In the morning and in the evening, engulfed in Nathan's pain and mine, carrying his frail and beautiful body which I could not fix, begging to be able to convey healing through my skin. "If you go away. Please don't go away."

I remember little of what the pediatric cardiologist brought in to ICU said to me, all compassion and quiet humility. I remember only, "I think he has an abhorrent left coronary artery." And so it was. Nathan had had a heart attack which had left his heart irreparably damaged.

I had paced the floor in emergency with Nathan draped over my shoulder the night before. Something was wrong. Our pediatrician had said he might hospitalize him after winter was over, as he was not thriving. But winter was not over, and here we were. He did not whimper or complain, but this time he was overcome. Nathan was not in the ward where I had left him as a failure-to-thrive baby the night before. I rushed to the nurses' quarters. "In ICU," they told me, pointing. By now I was desperate. This was all much bigger than life had prepared me for. I was not allowed to touch him. I was beginning to learn the meaning of the word anguish. "Ne me quitte pas." "If you go away. Please don't go away."

In the three-and-a-half years we shared after that, we crossed that bloody bridge together more times than I can count, pacing back and forth between death and life. Nathan said his first word in that ICU ward. The cardiologist had wrapped colored beads around his stethoscope. As I talked to Nathan about them, he smiled and said, "pretty," just like that, clear and complete. No baby talk from Nathan.

"It is good that you are pregnant again," the cardiologist had told me. Whatever did he mean? "He will not live through adolescence," he gently informed me a year later. And the lump in my throat grew to giant size.

"Ne me quitte pas." "If you go away. Please don't go away."

But he did. And I miss him still.

NAPOLEON

The Disney tale that was loved best by my sons was entitled *The Aristocats*. This tale held pride of place in their bedroom when they were tiny. Illustrated books accompanied the vinyl records of these tales. Nathan and Luke read-along and were consequently able to read unaided by the time they were three years old, ultimately without the support of the deeply mellifluous voice. The large black grooved circular disks filled their room with delight.

The Aristocats is the story of a retired old lady who willed all her possessions to her four cats. Her greedy butler kidnapped the cats, until a group of retired army dogs and a stray cat dared to stand in his way. Fantastic aristocratic adventures of cats and dogs and other animal friends followed, wherein the Bloodhound Napoleon stopped, puffed out his chest, deepened his doggy voice, and proclaimed to one and all, but particularly to Lafayette the Bassett Hound, "I'm the leader. I'll decide." There was something appealing in the bombasity of that statement, so my boys laughed each time they listened and mimicked Napoleon's voice and words at every possible opportunity. They still cannot resist the same when the situation warrants it. "I'm the leader. I'll decide," one of them will proclaim, and we will burst into laughter at the memories.

By the end of my first year of college I was ready for a break and an adventure. I had not heard of *The Aristocats*, but I was endeavoring to move into the mode of, "I'm the leader. I'll decide." It was decided that friend Jan and I would fly north to Sydney from Melbourne, and return by coastal ship. I made reservations for the flight and for our berths, and planned details regarding where we would stay and what we would do in Sydney. With no cell phones and no computers, the preparation was complicated and tedious, but my determination to move into a new stage of independence prevailed, and off we went.

In Sydney we met up with friends at a church camp. Their parents were extremely hospitable and invited a number of us to their farm after camp to enjoy country life for a few days. We drove trucks, picked fruit, traipsed around the paddocks, slept in, stayed up late, and drove into Sydney to enjoy the sights and sounds of the harbor and of Kings Cross. To us,

Sydney was a magic city—bustling and alive, and full of color and noise. It was a memorable contrast to Melbourne.

Jan and I had dressed up to travel on the plane—high heels, stockings with seams, tightly waisted dresses, and handbags. It was the thing to do. But shipboard life turned out to be by far the best part of the adventure. We knew we had hit the bigtime when we found ourselves conversing with the crew, who were dressed in their blinding white uniforms and looking both romantic and glamorous to a pair of seventeen-year-old girls. We felt grown-up and sophisticated eating at the captain's table and sailing the seven seas for three glorious days.

With Jan on our first big adventure.

For a few short days in my youth I felt like Napoleon, I was the leader and I decided.

*Leadership takes many forms in the paper bag of life. I was
awed to be an observer of this story of strength:*

THE POWER OF AN ORANGE

Two shining women sat
opposite each other
over coffee.
Mother and child,
they had loved each other well,
shared
many secrets.

Wondrous secrets
had entwined their hearts.
Secrets bound them
together,
in conspiracies
of glee.

Balm for the torments of life,
had long been
laughter.
Self-depreciating,
easy,
irreverent,
fulsome laughter.
By this,

life's bitter moments
were lightened.

But
this crucible of mother's pain
was particular,
exquisite agony.
It was weighted
by the knowledge
of her life imperiled.

They sat,
transported
by portents
of wordless grief.
Their hearts filled
with the tissue paper of hope,
as they stepped reverently
forward,
to unmask
and mock,
the consumer of life within.

Armed with years
of connecting joy,
and a valiantly rehearsed
new skill,
daughter offered ministrations

to her mother,
needle in hand.
"I have only practiced
on an orange,"
she whispered,
Rueful,
ashamed,
and embarrassed
by anxiety.

"Then," said Mother
head held high,
"I,
shall think,
like an orange!"

And with the courage
of a lighted torch
held into the dark,
she proffered
her arm.
Thin,
veined,
and shriveled with age.

And they laughed
again
in chorus.

Gleeful conspirators
in their valiant fight
for life.

CARDS

I wish I had kept them. Dozens of cards were delivered to my hospital room in Pensacola, Florida, along with a fusillade of flowers that bloomed their brilliant love and respect for me. When it was time for my release, the hospital loaned me a fat white van with a skinny white driver to transport those vases of flowers to a local seaside motel, where I was to stay and recover within the hospital's reach until I was well enough to lurch back onto life's merry-go-round.

The repeated message on those cards changed my life. That singular unified message was of such threatening reality that I was pulled into an orbit of unknowing by its impact. I did not understand it at all. The words had clanged and crashed around my hospital room. "It is time for you to look after yourself," they chorused, shattering me. I thought I had. I thought I was. I thought that looking after myself was a good idea. I exercised daily. I ate well. I had my nails done, kept my hair colored, grew colorful swathes of flowers in my garden, hugged the dog often, and kept stimulating company. But I could not escape the demand of the message there in my quiet hospital room, with a private nurse twenty-four hours a day in order to keep me hovering safely this side of eternity.

"It is time for you to look after yourself." I could not catch the true meaning by the tail. My mind was rendered as white as the driven snow. Blankness permeated. What was it that was so obvious to all who had written on those cards? It was a *sit up, take notice, and do something about it* kind of message, I was sure of that. More than sixty people stating it in chorus left me without cover.

I sat quiet and still in that motel room by the sea, and asked God to show me. A short time later I read this question: "How alive are you willing to be?" Hard on the heels of that question came a God-sent admonition, "You have learned how to perform. Now it is time to learn how to live." I was knocked naked. I felt exhausted. The courage required, alongside the fear of letting go, would require all of me, newborn. It would require physical, emotional and mental effort. If I did not hurry, I could miss my chance to be both fully human and fully alive.

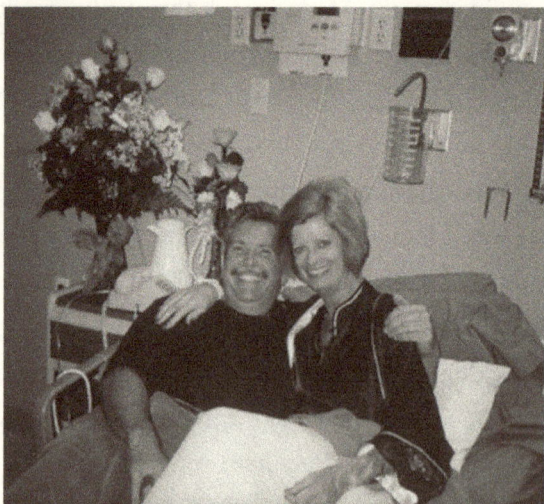

Griff, who drove me to emergency and would not hear of me sleeping on "those hospital sheets."

ENT specialist Thomas Schneider, who saved my life.

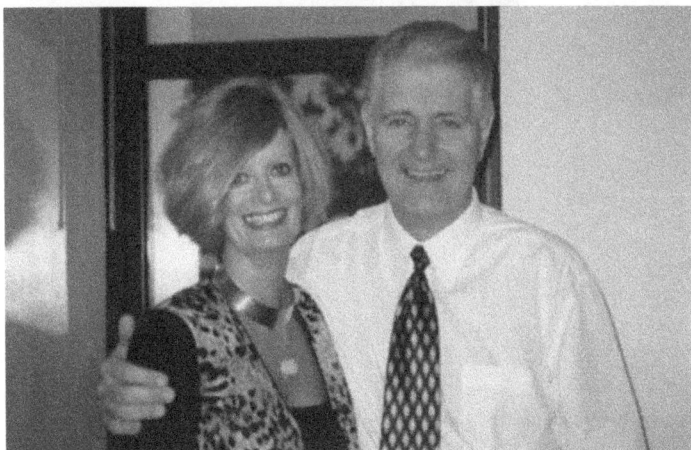

Patrick Madden, Sacred heart CEO, who also saved my life. When I asked him later why they had all worked so hard on my behalf, he said, "You were too young to die."

Anne Cooey, who also saved my life.

Beach at Pensacola, Florida. Made for healing.

In the paper bag of that motel room, with the sea offering life and light, I was granted the sweet medicine of laughter.

HELL NO

I opened
to her pert knocking
at my door.
In that magic moment
as I opened
to allow her
into my room,
she knew.
She knew,
why the flowers,
vibrant tokens of love,
filled every corner.

"You got married!"
she exclaimed.
Excited,
gleeful,
and genuinely thrilled
for me.
She was certain.
"You got married!"
she exclaimed
again,
face shining
with joy.

Her hair was frizzy
and sparse.
Tufts of it
sprouted
halo-like,
around the band of ribbon,
which crowned her head.
Her eyes were dark.
Her movements spry.
She knew.
She just knew.

"Hell! No!" I thought.
"Not married.
Not yet.
Not married.
Not this day.
Not this time.
Not this place.
Hell. No!"

But,
"Hell, no!"
did not easily
fall
from the lips
of a religious sprite
like me.

"Hell, no!"
did not drip
from my lips.
Someone raised
to look good,
be good,
think good,
and act good.

Whatever good was,
I was
well-practiced,
and well-rehearsed,
a seriously learned woman
in the ways
of good.

So, "Hell, no!"
I did not say.

"Well,
no."
I whispered,
pondering,
deliberate.
"I have just come out of hospital.
I was four hours
from death,

they say."

Whatever she thought,
my saucy helper,
she said
not another word,
but moved
silently,
past me
into the bathroom,
to ruminate and to clean,
while I moved
seriously
and slowly,
towards the window
to assess
the ocean
and it's power
to hold me
to a new
level of calm
and contemplation.

To heal me.

Then she appeared again,
tufts sprouting,
eyes shining.

"I know!"
she exclaimed.
"You had a baby!"
Her certainty.
Her joy,
and her wickedly
inaccurate assessment,
kept me going
for days.
It may
keep me going
for years.
She had absolutely
no interest
in the real story.
There was not
one question
in her mind.

She was happy
for me.
Very happy.

HOBNAILED BOOTS

A southern gentleman tramped endlessly across my anxious heart with his careless hobnailed boots as I drove Route 66. He was an exuberant and fascinating raconteur, large of both body

and intelligence, filled to the top with a mesmerizing personality, and Clinton-like in a charming Southern way. I loved his
stories. "Published in the *New Yorker*," he said proudly. And
they were.

"I love you," he told me again and again. He was larger than
life, and dangerous. He hurt people, and he did not care. His
life moved along, blithe and unsoiled. Others were left limp-
ing, hiding from their own pain and confusion. I knew this,
because he told me so.

Willis used to sit at the end of my bed to tell me stories
when I was a child. He held no book in his hand. He was never
published in the *New Yorker*. He had never read the *New
Yorker*. But the stories written in his heart and in his mind
never disappointed. He told stories of Bonnie and Floss, his
sheep dogs. My heart yearns still for their wriggle and lick and
their singularly intelligent eyes that I only ever experienced
in my imagination. They were alive to Willis, and I could see
them clearly in my mind. Every dawn in his youth, Willis
would creep out of bed, push his freezing feet into hobnailed
boots and run out into the frosty mist with Bonnie and Floss,
in a frantic attempt to save newborn lambs from the crows
which flew down, black as nightmares, to pick out their newborn eyes. I did not like to think about the picked-out eyes.
Silence covered the pain of my heart's imaginings.

Willis told me stories of Moratai, of Balikpapan, and of
Borneo—of the war fought by him for three years in order to
save Australia from a Japanese invasion, and me in particular from becoming a waitress in a Japanese restaurant. I knew

by heart the names of the village children he befriended. He showed me their photographs. I have them still. He told me stories about patient hours spent with Sid the monkey, coaxing him down the tent pole with food, and ultimately onto his shoulder to bring a smile to all the weary troops inside the tent. It brought a smile to my face, and Willis was enlivened in the remembering. "You can train any animal with food," he told me. I loved that monkey and wished I had met him.

Willis told stories of the endless sameness of the rations metered out to the Australian troops for all those years in the jungles of Papua New Guinea. "Bully beef," he would say, an edge of disgust in his voice. "Bully beef, every day, every meal. It sinks down into your stomach like a grave." My mouth would water up in sympathetic disgust. "And those dog biscuits! A dog wouldn't eat them! Break your dentures they would." I could feel my teeth cracking and crumbling at the thought of *those biscuits.*

"*But the mosquitoes!*" this said with his big Willis hand held out, thumb and forefinger extended. "They were enormous and mean. Talk about guerilla warfare! They would clomp across our chests in the middle of the night with their hobnailed boots, turn over our dog tags, check our blood type, and have a discussion—all before they would deign to bite any of us. Cunning little blighters!" he would grin. He would giggle then, and smile at me with the memory of it and in pleasure at his own sense of humor, and tuck me into bed with a quick, whiskery kiss. Willis's pain, carried home from the war, slunk dark and close to the ground, hiding from itself. Hiding from us. Silent.

He spoke of the horror decades later, and that only after I had had the temerity to ask. I had been afraid Willis would die before I knew, and his body had gone very still with the remembering. His deep blue eyes looked hard at me and off into the middle distance at the same time. It was as though he was riveted to a place I could not see. As he told me stories of unendurable suffering, he also told me that one night, hundreds of Japanese marched past the drainage ditch where he and his companions lay shivering and filthy on the side of the road. "They were so close we could smell them," he said. "We thought we would die. They tramped on and on, mortally close, and all we could hear was our beating hearts and the endless rhythm of the thump, thump, thump of their hobnailed boots."

Bonnie and Floss—Willis's farm companions, with an odd farm cat or two. The cats did not rate a story.

The southern gentleman who had mesmerized me and made me laugh, ultimately made me cry as he tramped across my heart with his hobnailed boots. He had requested a meeting, and three of us had met in my California office, where he invited me to join the gentlemen for lunch. His conversation was dazzling. He riveted me with his personality and endless funny stories. We enjoyed food that was fresh and plentiful, and wine as mellow as the California sun. Then he shocked me by offering, "A date tonight? There is no one in my life right now and I am looking for someone like you." He was so sure of himself.

The next day he called. "Take the afternoon off," he commanded, and I did. "You have to have a memory," he said, and bought me a multi-stranded amethyst necklace and gorgeous clothes—and flew home the next day. Big bunches of flowers arrived. Then I heard nothing until he called to say he was coming to California again. I was pleased to hear from him, but surprised when he proffered a black-and-white photograph of himself he wanted me to have, telling me to hold on for whatever would be next. He bought me more extravagant gifts and called after lunch to tell me that he had had fun with me and that it was just perfect and wonderful. He called from the airport when he got home and thanked me for our time together. But there was a growing watchfulness in my soul.

Suddenly it was June and he was in town again, and he came to see me. A few weeks later one of life's dramas caught me by the throat. I was fired, and I called to let him know. "I will call you back in three hours," he promised, and he did. He had thought of me a thousand times in the last week. He had gotten himself into a bit of a mess.

"Will you tell me what mess?"

"I got married!" he said. He had sat on my couch on Friday. He had married on Tuesday. I had been duped. I had also been rescued.

He had been so generous, but he had stolen a part of my soul. It was not that he got married. It was that he did not tell me. "I love you," he would whisper at the end of each call. Did he do this to every woman he met? Does he—now?

*There have been times when I have had to open my paper bag
of life to discernment regarding the meaning of love
and its possible consequences.*

TOO MUCH LOVE

Billy was a tiny student of mine during my Chicago years. He was the fourth of six children, beloved of his family, and a cute three-year-old button. Billy had a congenitally profound hearing impairment, and was learning to make use of his hearing aids and his smidgen of residual hearing. He was on the edge of beginning to comprehend that things have names. Every creative bone in my body came to bear to encourage Billy into the joy of language. Among all the cutting and pasting and music and color in our classroom, there were carrot tops growing, tiny turtles turtling, and fish being fish.

After months of puzzled concentration on Billy's part, his

family's close involvement, and my encouragement, one precious day a light bulb lit up his cherubic face. "Fish," he said, pointing. The sisters raced in from their classrooms and we clapped and cheered, as the light on his little face grew brighter with revelation. At home Billy's family gathered to hear him say his first word. More clapping and cheering encouraged more repetition. "Fish," said Billy, again and again. Off the whole family trotted to the nearest pet shop to buy a fish of Billy's choosing, and a fish bowl also of Billy's choosing, and fish food for Billy's own fish.

Billy continued to say "fish" as often as he could get anyone to pay attention. He watched his fish swim and swim and swim. Around and around it went, while on and on Billy said, "Fish," to the accompaniment of joyful clapping and cheering. Billy loved his fish. For days he did little else other than watch it swim, feed it, and say, "Fish." He loved his little fish so much that he took it carefully from its bowl, made a tiny fish bed, and tucked it in to rest, with a tiny fish blanket. Poor little fish. Way too much love.

My sister always said that kissing Thomas goodbye after breakfast was like kissing Flipper. Each morning he arranged a tidy supply of kippers onto his toast and consumed them with relish. He desired that I would love those stinky little fish as much as he did. My heart raced, but not with desire for kippers. I was looking for the nearest exit.

And then there was the man I met one fine Hawaiian morning as we found ourselves side by side in Waikiki's superb aquarium. Originally established in 1904, it is the second oldest operating public aquarium in the United States. Built as an attraction to entice travelers out from the city of Honolulu by trolley car along the beaches to Queen Kapiʻolani Park, it had grown into the world-class offering we were both enjoying. We were standing side by side, separated by no more than ten inches, yet he was focused elsewhere. After a little time, I spoke to him quietly. He turned and peered at me as if in a dream.

I had watched him as he tried to capture a photograph of a fish with his cell phone. His prey was elusive, giving the appearance of trying to hide in a corner between the glass observation screen and the side wall. After snapping a few shots, my companion breathed a resigned sigh. He was softened by some inner life. I spoke cautiously as he inclined his head. "I think it is trying to hide from you," I said, smiling at him.

A puzzled look flitted across his face until a sliver of understanding sent a ray of light to his eyes. The realization that I was there so close beside him and that we were concentrating on the same thing brought a gentle smile to his serious face. He leaned in, a conspirator now, "I donated that fish," he pointed, quietly proud and pleased.

"You did?" In all of my life I had not met one single person who had donated a fish—to anything. I worked hard to hold my mouth to attention and behave itself so that not even a tiny bubble of laughter escaped. This was serious business—everything about this gentleman's behavior told me that. "You did?" I inquired again, inviting more information.

Each time I am in Honolulu I visit this aquarium. It restores my soul. And we were here together, strangers, yet beginning to establish an intimate relationship over a fish. This was a small creature, only about six centimeters long, its lithe little body divided—red at the back and black at the front. In this place so filled with wonder it was pert and perky, but not outstanding. With more gentle probing I found out that this particular fish was of an endangered species, yet was still able to be purchased in pet shops. When my new friend had purchased this colorful darting baby, he had not planned to keep it. It had always been destined for this aquarium, where it would be studied and cared for, as any self-respecting fish would expect to be.

"Was your fish hiding from you just now?" I asked.

He looked at me in amazement. "Oh, no!" he replied. "It recognized my voice. They can recognize voices."

"What about all that pushing into the corner?" I asked.

"It was trying to get out to me, because it heard my voice. It knows me. I kept it for three years after I bought it. I had not intended to." My new friend was now opening his heart. He lowered his voice and leaned a little closer, filled with a gentle passion, "But I didn't know you could fall in love with a fish."

A fish to fall in love with in Waikiki Aquarium.

Oh, but I did.

FISH LOVE

It was the end of our writing class. Time had passed in a whiff of words and ideas, personalities and pleasure. I had just returned from a sparkling two weeks celebrating all things good in the sunshine of Queensland with my extended family, a swirl of food and bikinis, swimming pools and playgrounds, waking and sleeping, washing damp towels and making beds, nappies and breast-feeding—and the visiting of all kinds of birds and beasts. We had been to the Currumbin Bird Sanctuary to squeal with delight at the scratchy feet of the birds as they perched on our heads and arms. We had barbequed and shopped, clambered over boulders and swum against the tide in the river—swimming and swimming and staying in exactly the same spot. I was not much in the mood for anything but the loving. It had all been rather marvelous, the first time we had all been together for five years and I was basking in the pleasure of it.

My mind wandered back through my life, looking for a tale to tell. Many moons ago, in my youth, I had been taken to the drive-in movie theatre to see Alfred Hitchcock's movie, *The Birds*. I hated it and have never been the same since. I was terrified witless and could think of no sane reason why I would want to repeat such an experience. Ever. Could I write about that? When I was living in Providence, Rhode Island, I discovered that just down the street from my home was the Mafia headquarters where Raymond L. S. Patriaca holed up above an innocuous-looking dry cleaning shop. I thought of it every time I drove past but was too young and too naïve to be frightened by the knowledge. Almost every friend I had at that time was either involved in some way with the Mafia or had a close relative or friend who was. I did become frightened when I started getting "spook-me-out" phone calls at all times of the day and night, but I worked out who it was and called his bluff. Could I write about that?

Such memories, and I still could not catch a single thread to get me started on writing. The week wound its way through film class and book club, therapy at the Aquatic Center and coffee with friends, a movie at the Rivoli and Sunday lunch with the family. And then suddenly there it was. My big idea. Jan leant towards me as we sat at lunch and said she wanted to ask me a question. She launched right in. "Do you ever think of suicide?" she asked. The conversation was suddenly serious, with the torture in her head spilling over too much of the table and moving far too close to the children. Her naturally beautiful face was haunted as she struggled with her demons. She talked and talked until I managed to lead her gently to healthier pastures for her mind, and for mine. All the while, I was thinking here could be the threads for a short piece. We resumed an attempt at normalcy, and lunch was delicious.

Eventually young Kylie came to sit on my lap. Kylie was seven, cute and savvy, all long hair and sparkles and wobbly teeth and chatter. Our discussion roamed through stories of her new kitten's antics, the songs I used to sing to my boys when they were small, where her mother had bought her new sweater, and where she kept all her baby teeth after they had fallen out. We got to talking about loving, Kylie and I. Then on we moved to *generations*, a new word for Kylie, which she loved and kept using in sentences over and over, testing the feel of it in her mouth—the sound of it in her ears. Then on we went again, talking about loving her oldest grandmother, who was ninety-six years old.

Then on we went again, to death, and how Kylie thought it was sad when you had a funeral after your dog died. "Oh, yes," I said, all full of the wisdom of the ages, "it is always sad when a pet dies."

"Well," said Kylie with a dismissive sigh, "it is hard to be sad when a fish dies, because they do not last very long."

"Oh?" I responded, well admonished. But relentless in my desire to impart some modicum of wisdom into the pretty little mind, I went on, "There may be some people who love their fish."

"It is just hard for me to love fish!" she finished, shrugging.

I was finished too. I had threads and memories and stories to tell, but mostly I just wanted to sit with Kylie and let her tell me again that she found it hard to love a fish.

REFLECTIONS ON DAWGS

Willis had two dawgs, Bonnie and Floss. I met them in my imagination when he told me stories of "the farm." I had Penny when I was growing up, a sweet-natured bitzer (a bit like a dachshund and a bit like a collie and a bit like anything you like). But we loved him and he loved us. Penny slept outside in a wooden kennel Willis made, on an old hessian sack. That's what dogs did in those days in Australia. They were for "outside," and Penny was too. Except for the afternoon when he wandered into the kitchen when Merle was in the throes of preparing afternoon tea for a group of brethren ladies. Merle had a tea trolley, a wooden contraption with an upper and lower shelf that could be moved from room to room on its four metal castors. It was only ever used on special occasions. On the bottom shelf of the tea trolley Merle had placed a plate of tiny ham sandwiches cut into fingers, as was the fashion of the day. Penny liked that fashion. He liked the ham too, and swiped most of them before they were ever wheeled into the living room for the ladies who were all sitting primly, wearing their afternoon tea hats with little veils.

Every morning Penny went off for a walk, collecting dog friends along the way. The troupe wandered off for a few hours, returning by early afternoon unharmed and unmolested. It was the norm in those days to see small gatherings of canine friends roaming the streets, poking their noses into other people's business. Penny did have a collar but never a leash; he just followed along if we went for a walk.

Years later, when Luke began to show a fear of dogs, I bought Tommy. The people next door named their dog Tommy too, because they liked the name we had chosen. Tommy was a Cardigan Corgi, a sweet-natured doggy joy. He could play a mean game of soccer by himself, flipping the ball up into air with his nose and bolting to catch it before it hit the ground.

He chased along the inside of our fence as locals walked by, snarling and snapping but never did snarl or snap when the gate was opened. When visiting a friend in Oklahoma I laughed because he had two big holes cut into his side fence, where the Australian sheep dogs he kept would poke out their heads to keep their doggy eyes on the neighborhood goings-on. When I inquired about the holes he said that his dogs also barked and barked at any passerby. Once he cut the holes and they could see what was going on in the outside world, they never barked at passersby again. I

With my dawg, Penny.

do wish I had been smart enough to do that with Tommy. It would have saved a lot of traumatized walkers.

DAWG FANTASY

It was October again, and the dog was not happy. Not one little bit. In fact, the dog was so mesmerized by his deeply felt depression that he deposited his small furry butt right down on the footpath in the middle of what had been, until that moment, a brisk morning walk. All his life he had been known as Dawg. Even when he was little, although at that time he was Little Dawg, such as in "come here, little dawg," or "what a cute little dawg." But it had morphed into Dawg as he grew, and there it stayed.

It was not only late-October, it was also the late-October of his life—and the dawning realization that his childhood had well and truly rushed past him and right on through his kennel door could no longer be pushed from his doggy mind. He was tortured by aches and pains in every joint of what had been his pert doggy body. His eyelids seemed to have taken on a downward droop which all the twisting and turning of his doggy head did not seem to alleviate. Not one little bit.

"Not one little bit." These words reverberated through his doggy mind while threatening clouds hovered over his head. His childhood had suddenly up and gone, and he did not know where to find it. Up until now he had not thought about childhood or being a child or even acting in a childlike manner. But now, today, he was mesmerized by that which no longer existed for him. Where could it have gone? He tried again and again to remember if he had seen his childhood fleeing down some country track. But try as he might, he could not recall its departure. It was just gone. And with no warning. Nothing had caused him to worry that it might ever go. He just did not think about it at all. Up until now. And now he could think about nothing else. He was mesmerized. All his hopes and wishes for the next twenty years had fled with his precious childhood. He was taken aback.

Birds and beasts of all kinds can bring joy
in this paper bag of life.

TOUGH TURKEY

Christmas was coming to my corner of southern California, and I was offered a gift of a beautifully printed, gold-embossed certificate which was redeemable at Stater Bros. Supermarket for one frozen turkey of between eight and twelve pounds. Sounded a bit skinny to me, but it was free. Having been known in the dim and distant past for my ability to cook, and having been known in my more recent past for my lack of interest, desire, or passion for cooking, I decided that I would make it up to all my friends. It would be to my benefit and theirs that I should wander off to Stater Bros. to choose my free, skinny turkey. I would dust off my cooking prowess, cook, slice, and offer the poor bird—and in the doing would save so much money that I could endow my favorite charity forever, as well as providing myself with such small practical items as another Mercedes and big diamonds. This turkey could become my ticket to financial freedom as well as the resurrection of my reputation as a cook.

To-market-to-market I went. Carried home triumphantly, the turkey was thawed, separated from its giblets and stuffed to perfection with my secret mix, using three golden orbs from my orange tree, which I thought to be an exotic touch. My mind roamed from California to Middle America—and to Mal, who owned an enormous turkey business that he eventually sold to Sarah Lee. "How did you become involved with turkeys?" I had asked he who knew much about these ugly feathered friends. His blue eyes lit up as he grinned at me. "I was scratching for a living," he confided.

Up to 500 degrees went my oven and in went the poor, dead, undernourished bird. Placed in a searing-hot oven to start, the outside would be crisped and the inside left tender, succulent, and full of mercy. I turned on the oven light and, looking in, felt inordinately proud of my accomplishments thus far. Off I went to work in another part of the house, only to be accosted thirty minutes later by veil of grey, strong smelling smoke and a prancing dog. I bolted for the kitchen. I had forgotten to turn the oven down from the 500 degrees! Billowing black smoke filled every corner of the kitchen and was pouring ominously and energetically from all the oven vents.

I rushed to open the windows, turn on the exhaust and ceiling fans, and open the oven door. But this seemingly harmless door now imprisoned the poor ugly beast within, it was stuck fast, tightly closed, and not about to budge. From the corner of my eye I caught sight of that turkey, my erstwhile ticket to financial freedom, enthroned on the oven rack and staring balefully at me through the murk, sizzling and spurting and splattering fat with abandonment.

Why in the world couldn't I get the door open? I discovered the next day that the very handle I had so very carefully pulled across, was the handle used to start a self-cleaning process in the oven! Up until now I had not used this oven in my California nest. It had remained very clean while I dined out or purchased takeaway. There sat my turkey, engulfed in smoke and suffering the indignity of being self-cleaned while my visions of a new Mercedes and big diamonds wafted out the kitchen window with the smoke. By then, it was midnight, and I could not think of a thing to do except to turn the oven off, and hope that the turkey would be in a more affable mood in the morning.

Morning—and the turkey looked, well, cooked and reasonable. The oven, on the other hand looked cooked and unreasonable, encrusted with blackened turkey fat which was splattered from one side to the other. The kitchen smelled like serious food production and the dog was desperate. It was a miracle that I could move the handle back, and that I could open the oven door at all. I sliced and ate a few pieces, gave some to the dizzily grateful dog, and put the rest of the great beast into the refrigerator. There it sat sullenly for two days until I decided I did not want anything more to do with it, and gave it away.

The oven, however, was still filled with its drippings and droppings. So to Stater Bros. I repaired one more time to purchase myself a can of odor-free oven cleaner. Home I came and started to spray. The dog, gagging and gasping, rushed around the house in a frenzy of chemical overload. I closed the oven door and put the can away. Two days later I paid my cleaning lady twenty dollars to finish cleaning my self-cleaning oven.

There must be a lesson there somewhere. My best offering at this time is: "When you come to visit me next, let's go out to eat."

AMERICAN FOOD

"And what would you like for breakfast this fine day, my son?" I asked, patting his head gently.

"Apple pie," said Toby, smiling his winsome three-year-old smile. That pulled my smoothly gliding morning to a stop. I hesitated just enough to draw in a motherly "mother knows best" kind of breath, leaned over that tow-haired boy, and breathed sweet nothings into his cute little ear.

"I can offer you pancakes, or waffles—pancakes with syrup, waffles with bacon and syrup. I can offer you crunchy granola bars. I can offer you toast. I can offer you toast with peanut butter, jam, or honey. There is toast with nothing. Toast with eggs?"

"Apple pie," Toby replied, unperturbed. "I would like apple pie for breakfast."

I looked hard at him for a minute before laughing out loud. "Why not!"

> *The breaking of bread together is the*
> *stuff of life in this paper bag.*

ORANGES IN NEW YORK

Arthur Miller's play, *A View from the Bridge*, tells of the wonder and disbelief of a New York lass of Italian heritage when she is told that in Italy, oranges grow on trees. She is first disbelieving, then excited. A fine play, it is a triumph of Miller's disciplined mind and social conscience. I was transported back to New York City as I enjoyed the production at the Sumner Theatre in Melbourne.

My friend Dina was born in New York of Italian heritage. We had met in Bermuda where we had both been on retreat. We took one look at each other, recognized a little wickedness, and escaped the retreat down to a beachside restaurant where we ate lobster, drank champagne, and shared stories of our lives. Dina told wonderful tales of growing up in New York with Poles, Greeks and Italians—each group taking up residence in their own area, together but divided.

When I returned to New York with Mr. T, Dina took us to what was her late husband's favorite restaurant, Gino's. Now closed after sixty-five years of service to A-listers and everyman, it had been a place where her husband had hobnobbed with colleagues, as well as the likes of Frank Sinatra and Tony

Bennett. For many, it was their favorite New York restaurant of all time.

Famous it was. Glamorous it was not. When we arrived by cab, we had to clamber through what looked like a construction site.

But the walls inside were covered in glorious red and black Scalamandre Zebra wallpaper with three hundred and fourteen leaping zebras. All items on the menu had been handwritten in ink sixty years before by the restaurant's founder, Gino Circiello. The same twenty-seven tables and seventy-four chairs graced the room as had when it was first opened.

The Italian waiters had seen it all. Some were purported to have spent all their working lives in that place. Dina told me with a smile that they absolutely would not engage. Undaunted, I drew on years of practice and as much charm as I could muster until, eventually, I drew a story or two from our stony-faced and grumpy waiter. He told me tales of the 1950s, when immigrants from all over Europe were entering the US via New York, both legally and illegally. Girls were desperate to stay, and the waiters were happy to assist. Marriages took place right there in Gino's every ten minutes, with the waiters collecting fifty dollars from each hopeful girl, "marrying" again and again and again each day.

There is interesting food in the paper bag of life.
Interesting people too.

FOUR MISSING WORDS

I was waiting.

Guests had come in from all over the US for a special evening of celebration in southern California. Every single person who had been invited had come—from as far away as Beaumont, Texas; Palm Beach, Florida; New York; and Washington State. One man even flew in from Australia. Down the freeways and over the hills they came—across the country, as eager as the little bear that went over the mountain to see what he could see.

I had welcomed them all and now was waiting outside for our honored guest. All my preparations had been made with scrupulous care. The press had been informed. The caterer I had used many times. Silver domes would be removed in unison with military precision. Sumptuous food would be offered. No clattering dishes or clanking cutlery would be heard; there would be no intrusion of any kind. Security was at the ready. Campus lights were blazing. Hair was coiffed. Best speaking voices were prepared. Suits were pressed and ties straightened. The tables were marvelous.

Finally, the word came through to me that our guest was on his way, walking in stately unison across the campus with our CEO. I was so ready that all I had to do was wait. But no, I thought—to be on the safe side I must call security one more time to confirm their last instruction. "Our guest has requested that no one approach him while he is eating. Understood?"

"Yes, Ma'am."

"Please do not approach him while he is eating."

I moved to the side of our guest at the lobby door. His interpreter was the best I had ever seen, so brilliant that we were able to walk and have an effortlessly fluid conversation without the usual hesitation between languages. Up in the elevator we went, chatting like old friends, and into the room to meet the assembled throng of eager guests.

As we walked towards the receiving line for me to make introductions, the whole line began to move gracefully away from us as in a wave. They looked like a group of slow-moving synchronized swimmers. It took me but a quick breath and three seconds to perceive that something had gone terribly wrong.

I looked inquiringly and desperately at the nearest friend, stately blonde Miss Marcia from Beaumont, Texas, and whispered hoarsely, "What the …?"

"We were informed by security," she said, waving her arm along the receiving line, "on no account to approach him!" Sotto voce, eyebrows arched, and underlining every single word in full Texan—she continued, "We were told on NO account to approach him."

Those four little words, "While he is eating," got totally left out in the midst of security's nervous preparations. "On no account approach our guest *while he is eating*," had been my instruction. "Please move in here and let's get thing this started!" I breathed, pointing in front of me. And bless Miss Marcia, she did, and we were off and running. "This is Mr.

Harry Thomas. He is from Dallas, Texas, his businesses are …
etc., etc., etc."

The evening went well. Speeches were interesting and
appropriate. Food and service were excellent, and those who
had the chance for a private photograph with our honored
guest were glowing. With dinner and speeches over, back
along the hallway we went, down in the elevator, and across
the campus to the waiting limousine. And then, while I was
standing formally gracious and appropriate—suddenly and
unexpectedly, he leaned forward and hugged me. Tight.

"Thank you, darlink," he purred into my ear.

Four little words had gotten lost earlier—and so, nearly,
had my equanimity.

But now? He hugged me. Tight!

Mikhail Gorbachev hugged me!

Mikhail Sergeyevich Gorbachev, his daughter Irina
Mikhailovna Virganskaya, and me.

My paper bag of life has been filled with surprises.

AND THEN THERE WAS CHUCK

It was sunset and I was into winding down—thinking of a glass of wine and a little relaxation. I had been no more than three weeks into my new position in California when there was a call from my CEO. "I have an invitation which I am unable to make use of, Jillian. I am wondering if you would take my place?"

"Of course!" I was there to do the bidding of the great man. To aid and abet, to uphold and encourage. To please and to remind. To cover and complement. To be all things. Of course, I would go. What was it, and when was it?

"It's an event to be held at the Beverly Hills Hotel, Jillian. It starts in two hours."

"Tonight?" I queried, a little daunted. Drive home, clean up and glamorize, then a one-hour drive on the Los Angeles freeways? I could just about manage it.

"The invitation is for two people, Jillian. You may choose to invite someone to join you if you wish."

"May I ask about this event?"

"It is to be a reception to be hosted by Charlton Heston."

"Did you say Charlton Heston?"

"I did."

I opted to invite Casey, who was up for almost anything. As Hollywood gorgeous as we could manage, we set off on our adventure, grinning. Casey had attended Hollywood High in

her youth, so the trappings were a little more familiar to her than to me. At Mac Robertson Girls High School in Melbourne town we did not much run into celebrities. We were more likely to run into subject mistresses flapping down the hallways in their academic robes.

The hotel loomed warm and welcoming, and we were ushered into the gathering with quiet grace. There were about twenty of us who were served particularly fine food, including tiny grilled Australian lamb chops that I chose to believe Charlton had ordered in especially for me. The guests were mostly reporters, except for the one plastic surgeon who gave me his card and offered me his services, checking out every corner of my visage as he did so.

Casey came along with me with the express purpose of taking my photo with Charlton. As I did not expect I would meet with him very often she had been given clear instructions. This was why she was here. This was her job. She was a good photographer, after all. The evening went swimmingly, and Casey did maneuver her way between the madding crowd to flash away with her camera. Charlton presented us each with a beautifully boxed DVD of *Voyage through the Bible*, which he was launching. As he signed mine, Casey went to town with the camera.

We sat together by the log fire when it was all over to enjoy a glass of port before the trip home. We had had fun, and for the next hour, as we sat, we enjoyed waving to Charlton as he walked by us—once, twice, three times. We were old friends by the time the evening ended, but I did have to resist the urge to straighten his toupée.

Only trouble was, when Casey produced the developed photographs, something had gone awry. There was Charlton in all his good-looking glory, and there was my nose! Jillian's nose was glowing beside Charlton Heston. So much for my Hollywood days.

My nose with Charlton Heston.

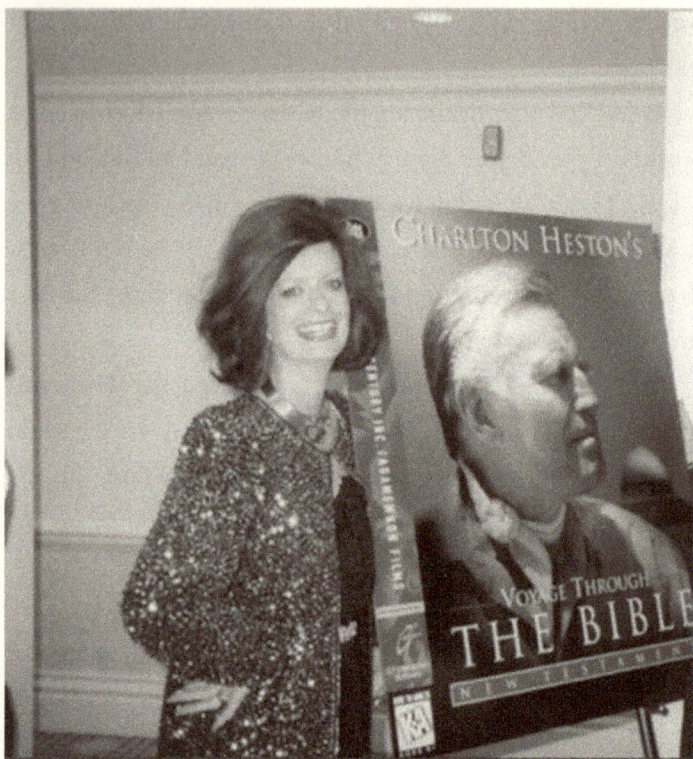

Making up for it.

November 8, 1995

Dear Mis Morey:

Thanks for your warm letter and kind
comments; it was good of you to take the time and
trouble to write me so generously.

It was lovely of you to come to the launch
of VOYAGE THROUGH THE BIBLE. I must say, I think
it has come out very well, thanks to the
technicians who seem able to do magic on computers.
I hope you enjoy the finished product.

My best wishes to you and all good luck.

Happy Thanksgiving!

Showing off after my time with Charlton Heston in the Beverly Hills Hotel.

Men can be tough on a girl trying to keep alive
in the paper bag of life.

PINK BOOTS

When I was growing through to womanhood, a man was considered to be the head of the household and everything else. A woman was expected to submit to a man, whether he was the head of their household or not. Women who dared say nay would suffer. Women were not free to think for themselves or, God forbid, to speak for themselves. I am older now, and I will make no more sacrifice at the altar of such male arrogance. A crazy-maker I knew when I was young almost succeeded in making me crazy with anger, grief, and frustration. "You cannot ask the reason why," he had intoned. Imperious, intol-erant, and standing carefully with an, "I know better than you" kind of stance, he had stamped his highly polished leather boot on the pavement. "You will just be frustrated if you ask the reason why," he stamped, righteously determined that I should heed his warning.

I listened and nodded, for I thought him to be wiser than I. Years passed, and when we headed into that conversation again, I was tougher and smarter. So I said, "I can, you know, and I will." He was not pleased at all. But suffering had made me less afraid. I was braver and bolder and louder. I had found a shaft of light, and with it came enough sanity, hope, and courage to sustain me on a new path with no name. My life had been void of stories with any moving-forward component, and I had felt sitting-down, sucking-my-thumb kind of stuck—not able to see past my own shadow. I could not see over the top of my paper bag of life, the side was too high for me to find the first foothold. I needed the shocking clarity of fresh insight and bite-sized pieces of life-giving wisdom. I needed light on the path for my hesitating foot. I needed to vitalize my courage, increase my hope, and expand my vision.

"I will ask the reason why, and with sanity restored I will be out of the paper bag. Take your patronizing hand from my shoulder. Put your highly polished boot right back where it belongs. This is my private and perilous journey. I will take a good dose of courage and turn over the soil of my mind. No old bones here. Just the soft fresh smell of earth ready for spring. Don't mess with me. Soft tears have washed the muddied windscreen of my mind. I will put on my own boots, my outrageous bright cerise-colored boots, thigh-high and suede, with marvelously high heels.

"I can hardly walk in them. But they are exactly what I need for my journey."

Shoes can be as armor for a girl in this paper bag of life.

THE RED SHOES

When I left 45b Bowen Street, my parental home, at the age of twenty-two, my parents still had not owned a television set. Willis was scathing about the evidence of such godlessness, calling it "a sin box" in his typically conservative brethren way. Ironically, in his later life he relented and purchased a television that he loved and watched it reverently and often—possibly making up for his loss. He endeavored to keep his conscience calm by storing the offending sin box in a cupboard which could be opened with ease to offer him a full view from his olive-green reclining chair, or closed with ease to hide it from visitors. He realized that he could learn a lot through this medium, and as he had always been an avid reader and absorber of both useful and useless information, there was nothing quite so convenient as a television. He did not eat humble pie though; the sin box stage of his life was permanently erased from his mind once the joy of the screen was in front of him. He should have taken up selling them; he could have made a fortune.

I was taken to only one movie during my childhood. It was entitled *The Greatest Show on Earth*. That experience was so overwhelming that I felt ill, and I remember only that the enormous drama was far too much for my childish mind. When I saw a second movie, *The King and I*, I fell hopelessly in love with Yul Brunner, Deborah Kerr, and the whole cinematographic business: dancing, singing, romance, the whole bit. I am in love to this day. By the mid-1990s I was living in southern California, where Hollywood pervaded. I made many gratifying friendships there, one of which was with the still stunningly beautiful star of stage and screen Rhonda Fleming, who made more than forty films. Inside her Century City home, a wall that sweeps upwards alongside the staircase to the second floor is painted with a vast mural by one of Hollywood's premier set designers. The whole home has the look of set design, functional, beautiful, spacious, and filled with memories and love.

When I was recovering from life-saving surgery in the Sacred Heart Hospital in Pensacola, Florida, I spent some time talking with friends on my cell phone. The CEO of Sacred Heart, Patrick Madden, who came each day to check on my recovery, asked me once who I had been talking with. "That was Rhonda Fleming," I replied. "Do you know who I mean?" He looked at me totally taken aback.

"Are you sure?" he asked. When I assured him that I was, he told me a tale of unrequited love. His father's. Still living in Ireland, his father had been an adoring fan of Rhonda's for years.

"Would you like to speak with her?" I asked. He would, and I called Rhonda back and let them enjoy the story of her Irish fan of so many years. The upshot of all this fun was that I asked Rhonda to sign a publicity photo of herself and send it to Patrick to send on to his father as a surprise. The last time I saw Patrick he told me that his father still lives on his pleasure at the response of his drinking buddies as he goes from pub to pub producing Rhonda's signed photograph from his coat pocket.

A film I loved, but which frightened me from the first time I saw it, was *The Red Shoes*, produced in postwar London in 1948. The flame-haired Moira Shearer starred as Victoria Page. Born in Scotland in 1926, this was her first film role. It had been decided that dancers who could act would be chosen rather than actors who could dance. Rhonda Fleming and her Hollywood friends laughed at me often, telling me that I looked very much like Moira Shearer. This led me to looking for a photograph of Moira to see what they could see in me that reminded them of her. I did not remember that she had been the star in The Red Shoes and was astonished when I looked up her bio. Filmed on location in London, Paris, and Monaco, it is a Hans Christian Andersen tale come to life. It is said to have been inspired by the meeting of Sergei Diaghilev, who founded and was impresario of *Les Ballets Russes de Monte Carlo*, with British ballerina Diana Gould. Martin Scorsese names *The Red Shoes* as one of his favorite films. In a "play within a play" setting, in the film's final ballet scene depicting a half-destroyed London filled with both rubble and possibilities—the story ends in destruction, for the red shoes cannot be taken off, and they dance their wearer to her death. The film shows life to be dangerous, glorious, absurd, vivid, and terrifying in turn.

And so it has been for me in my paper bag of life.

WHO STOLE MY UNDIES?

Photo: kino-teatr.ru
Moira Shearer. Any resemblance to me? What do you think?

I was looking for a photo of Rhonda Fleming. Rhonda is a beautiful girl. As her sixth husband smiled into his coffee, his eyes crinkled in mirth and he glanced up at me with a twinkle to say, "Not too hard on the eyes, eh?" We both laughed. Rhonda's life and times were unknown to me until she came into Orange County, California to address a conference for women. I was there to take care of her. Her mellow voice tinged with the fragrance of warmed honey, she breathed glamour and confidence along with the expectation of deference.

Photo albums filled with the canned stories of my life beset me as I pick up one after another and turned the plastic-covered pages hunting for the photo of Rhonda that is as clear in my mind as if it was only just captured. I found photos of Hilde and my nephew Jayson, wed in Minnesota. I was not thinking of their wedding when I started to look. I found photos of me out and about in California. I found the photo of my nose alongside Charlton Heston. I found photos of me hosting a dinner for five hundred as a fundraiser for the Care Foundation, with George Schultz as honored guest. Preparation for this red carpet, black-tie dinner entailed the three months of my first summer in California.

I found photos of me escaping into the joys of Europe for the first time—Italy, Austria, and Germany. I found photographic memories of joyful moments caring for the multitude of Australian friends who came my way for a tour of greater Los Angeles—a bed, a dinner, and directions to take them safely back onto the freeways of Los Angeles and more shopping.

By then, I was dazed with the realization of how much work I had done in those six Californian years. But I still could not find the one photo I sought.

There was definitely something about Rhonda. At the sound of a camera shutter, her every womanly breath moved to concentration on posture, chin, chest, lips, and eyes—all of which come to her aid with professional poise. Over the years that followed and up until now, we have enjoyed precious moments, serious and searching, revealing and harsh, confronting and just plain fun. Rhonda laughs deeply, that honeyed throaty voice sending charm and ready good humor through space to land as a blessing on those in her company.

"When I first went to work with them, they asked me why I spoke in such a little girl voice," she told me. Walking down the street as a teenager, she had been spotted in true Hollywood style, taken to the studios, asked to read, and offered a part. "It is a true fairy tale," she still says. "They taught me then that I could lower my voice and even sing with a lower, mellower, sexier voice. Now," she says with a laugh, "this is me!"

That *me* demands attention even when not demanding attention. Her entry into any room causes a pause into which is dropped the fluttering of a whispered, "That's Rhonda," as observers point and smile at each other in satisfaction. I smile as I think of her. She is a woman given to good works, and her name is honored for the beneficence she bestows on the poor and downtrodden through her charitable works. Goodness and glamour define her, but she can never be misread as an easy touch. Life has caused her to be strong, and those who have taken from her without permission have built into her a steely grace. But I could not find the photograph I needed to tell my tale. I had taken photos of many of the interesting, idolized, zany, important and self-indulged I had met in my travels across the United States—and I knew that, among the many I had of her, there was one of Rhonda in Arizona, bravely clutching to her breast a set of fluorescent pink underwear of the prison variety. I had the ridiculous image in my head of bright pink prison-wear and smiling zanily for a camera. I needed the photograph to verify my memory, and I could not find it.

It is necessary at this stage of the proceedings to alert you to the fact that Rhonda has one of those Hollywood chests. It was well before the days of the "bosom-up" operations of today that she was spotted on the streets of Hollywood by a talent scout—and her bust is all her own, as are her deep voice, stunning red hair, and statuesque gorgeous self. As we lunched together in her home one time, she reached between her breasts and pulled forth her lipstick. "You did that?" I gasped with laughter.

"Oh, I always keep it here," she laughed back at me, "it's convenient."

Some time ago the news from the United States bleated out the fact that Trump had pardoned a certain Joe Arpaio, former sheriff of Arizona, for criminal contempt of court. The pardoning was painful for me to contemplate, given Joe's reputation for cruelty and racial profiling. I had raised my head to hear the news in anguish and astonishment when I realized that I had met this man.

He was the one who had offered the prison garb to Rhonda and me when we were on business in Arizona. The circumstances surrounding our meeting up with Joe Arpaio escapes me, as they were certainly not the primary reason for our visit to that state. What I did remember was his prideful telling of the tent cities he had established for the inmates of his prisons in Maricopa County, where temperatures have been known to reach 120 degrees. He was also proud to tell us that he was the toughest sheriff in America. As Rhonda and I attempted to comprehend his stories, he moved on to the newsworthy fact that he had mandated that all inmates were now required to wear bright pink underwear. With no knowledge of what is needed to run a prison filled with world-weary hardened criminals, I could do no more than say, "Wow." My knowledge of the harrowing situations he created came much later. I did not know then that he was proud of the indignities he caused his inmates.

He offered to show Rhonda and me a sample of the garish pink underwear. "Why give them a color they like?" he asked. There we were, each being offered a set of fluorescent-pink, prison-issue underwear. We took the proffered gifts and posed politely for the cameras. "I do not think I will use these," demurred Rhonda as she handed me hers. I believe we thanked him politely, as though he had bestowed us with true gifts.

I gave each of my boys a set. Perhaps they felt the shame sooner than I did, because they carry no memory of that gift.

I did find that photo of Rhonda sweltering away in Arizona, smiling for the camera, holding the bright pink evidence of the ignominy he bestowed upon his charges. As I watch Trump tweet to the governors of the US to "dominate" the peaceful protesters against police brutality, I understand why he pardoned Arpaio.

And I am traumatized by life in the paper bag of the US— filled far too full with division and fear and COVID-19. This is my other home, this nation that has in the past offered hope and promise to the poor and the needy. For sixteen years my life was challenged and formed there, and I will always be grateful. But today? I am sad.

In Arizona with pink undies.

Communication holds a key to this paper bag of life.

QUICKENING

He leaned across the table towards me, offering understanding. He was listening. He did care. I could see it on his face. As he spoke, I was instantly on alert, aware that I would have to become more adept at altering my idiom, my phrasing, and my general use of language if I was ever to connect in this most foreign of foreign countries, California. "It is difficult to make sexual connection here," he proffered solemnly.

I took in a short, shocked breath. He had totally missed my point. I was making observations about my first few weeks in California, and his empathetic reply whizzed right past my ears and disappeared out through the open door of my favorite southern Californian restaurant. My comment had been in relation to intimacy—intimacy as in connection in a new place. Intimacy as in feeling the gentle opening into possible friendship. Intimacy as in listening to the heart with the heart. Intimacy as in trust. I trust you and you trust me. But the very word *intimacy* placed copious opportunities for copulation into his head, and one more challenge into my hands. Issues of language can offer the opportunity to express with clarity an exactitude of thoughts, ideas or observations so that another may listen and sigh, "That is the way I would have expressed it, if I could." They can also be fraught with misunderstanding.

Returned to Australia to live in Melbourne town, this moment of missed communication came onto the screen of my mind as I walked down Swan Street, Richmond. At the corner where I needed to turn, my heart did a little flip of joy. As this had happened once before at exactly the same spot I was caused to halt and watch my heart and mind for a few precious moments. "'St. Crispin's St," said the blue street sign at the corner. An ordinary little sign it was, sitting at the corner of an ordinary little lane. None of the brave bluestone paving so common in Richmond adorned this streetscape. To my left a dark and desultory parking area abutted Domino's Pizza where two dirty and decidedly sad-looking motorcycles waited their turn to offer Uber Eats to the wider world. On my right, an abandoned two-story shop was groaning its way into a freshened-up existence. The row of scraggly trees that I had walked past for years had been cut down to ugly stumps, lined up in a row like petrified soldiers. Graffiti groaned its way over every surface the Richmond brats could reach.

Further down this little lane a young man of Indian or Sri Lankan descent leant against the plain red brick wall of the Richmond Library, telephone at his ear, one leg bent at the knee to prop up his body as he talked, taking a break from the slavery of delivering Domino Pizzas on one of those tired-looking motor bikes at the corner. The parking lot opposite the library's red brick wall was bordered by a profusion of weeds.

But my mind was back at the street sign at the corner—St. Crispin's St. And as I thought of it my heart did that little flip again. It felt similar to the quickening of a child in the womb, momentary and momentous all at the same time, and left me breathing shallow little breaths of wonder. "Why?" I thought. "Why with this name?"

Later I read again the Saint Crispin's Day speech from William Shakespeare's play, Henry V, in Act IV, Scene iii, 18–67.

> This story shall the good man teach his son;
> And Crispin Crispian shall ne'er go by,
> From this day to the ending of the world,
> But we in it shall be remembered;
> We few, we happy few, we band of brothers;
> For he to-day that sheds his blood with me

Shall be my brother; be he ne'er so vile,
This day shall gentle his condition:
And gentlemen in England now a-bed
Shall think themselves accursed they were not here,
And hold their manhoods cheap whiles any speaks
That fought with us upon Saint Crispin's day.

Here intimacy was birthed amidst battle-forged love. Rare moments, never forgotten, that caused quickening of both heart and body. And as I read those words again, my spirit quickened at the profound connection here expressed so eloquently.

VIRGINAL

He was so arrogant
that when I got off the phone
I wanted to go upstairs,
take a shower,
and put on my white dress.

Virginal.

Vestal virgins.
It's been a joke for years.
The pious ones,
their sins hidden.
The frightened ones.
The pretending ones.

The parsimonious,
sanctimonious ones.

I stood in front of a doctor once.
Naked.
"Virginal," he said.
"I don't think so,"
I thought.
"Three full term babies.
No,
not virginal."

I have a white dress.
I love it.
Soft fabric,
almost sheer.
Two layers.
Long.
Sleeveless.
Slit past the knee on each side.
Bias cut.
Simple.
Sexy.
A paradox.
A white dress,
but definitely
not virginal.

I loved to wear it.
Easy.
Sensuous.
Summery.
Dress it up.
Dress it down.

"Dry clean only,"
it said.
I washed it.
It shrank.
In cold water.
On gentle cycle.
and it shrank?
"Read the instructions.
Disobey at your peril."

I loved it.
I ruined it.
I grieve over it.
I will give it away.
I will have a new dress.

Everything
is for a season.
Even the best.
Even virginity.

I have learned to be careful in this paper bag if life,
and I will learn to be more careful as I continue to make
many small adjustments. So how do risk and
chance integrate with caution?

RUN AWAY—RUN AWAY

Annie had a glint in her eyes as she came to sit beside me, breathless with laughter. "I had a blind date on the weekend," she giggled. This was good news. Annie had been feeling lonely for some time. "He had such a yummy voice on the phone. He sounded really promising. I was excited," she confided. He of the yummy voice, she explained, was a well-known author of many books, in town to speak at a conference.

She spluttered through another giggle, "You need to know that the very best part of the date was when I put on my sparkly earrings." Now she had left me behind. What did that mean? "Well," she said, "I thought that the red sports car sitting outside the restaurant looked promising, but it turned out that it wasn't his. I was a bit disappointed, but I thought there would be more promise inside the restaurant." Seated waiting for her date, her sparkly earrings all aquiver, Annie started when someone tapped her gently on the shoulder. Gently? That felt good. Annie turned, as coyly elegant as she could manage, and looked up into an overwhelming sea of beige. There he was. Beige hair. Beige face. Beige shirt. Beige jacket. Beige slacks. Beige man.

"He sat down opposite me, and we perused the menu. By

now I was ready for real promise. I ordered a glass of wine. And guess what he ordered. Water!" she expostulated. "We tiptoed carefully through dinner, until by midnight I was way past ready to say goodnight. When he leaned towards me, I thought he was going to kiss me, but he handed me a large sealed envelope. It had been a bit of a long night, yet I was touched that he had thought to bring a gift on our first date. He wanted me to open it when I got home, and I thought that at last there was going to be an exciting part. I could hardly wait to see what was inside. It was a video, and I instantly hoped that it was An Affair to Remember with Deborah Kerr. Once I settled down for a good look, I realized that it was not a commercial video or a home video, but something professionally prepared."

By now Annie was slapping me on the shoulder, hardly able to stay on her seat she was laughing so much. "The video was the one he had played at his wife's funeral four years before!"

There are times in the paper bag of life when the only option is to pop out and run for your life.

IMMIGRATION

"What are you doing here?" asked the security guard, all po-faced determination.

"I've come to check the status of my immigration," I replied. I had done this before, waiting in line at the Immigration and Naturalization Service, first in Chicago years earlier, and now here in Laguna Niguel, California. This round had already been thirty-six months, and I was what Cheri called "land bound," her snooty little nose in the air, blue eyes snapping and shoulders shrugging. I could not leave the country. "Don't behave like that!" I fumed at her inside. "At issue here is my life, not yours!" Cheri had told me often enough that she had been seconded to me because she was a paralegal, but her attitude made me begin to think she could as well be labeled as a paranormal.

While walking on the beach in Florida with a friend four weeks earlier, Air Force jets had plunged through the sky overhead. He turned towards me, proud and happy. "What do they spell?" he commanded, pointing. "Freedom!" he proclaimed.

"They spell war to me," I thought glumly. What would freedom mean to me? To see my boys four times a year? To travel to amazing places all over the world? To dance?

I grimaced once over a cartoon depicting a man who was waiting alone to be served at a bank. Despite the fact that he was the only person waiting, he was forced to walk back and forth more than a dozen times between the meandering ropes in order to find his way to the service counter. A sign stated: Do not forget the ropes! No short cut was allowed. In these offices of the Naturalization and Immigration Service, I was fenced in on all sides by row after row of meandering red and blue ropes. Perhaps it was a patriotic thing.

The room was filled with lines of folk standing disconsolately on the loudly flecked linoleum, which had marks like tire marks emblazoned across it, right up to the wall. Did someone play weird games with cars in that room after dark—in that place of hopes and dreams? I was the only Caucasian in the room. It felt lonely. It was hard to connect. Cheri, the paranormal paralegal had been remote in her dealings with me. In this place, the security officers were remote. In the past few years, each time I returned from another country, customs officers were remote. Placed behind partitioned walls, the personnel here felt remote. As I stood and then shuffled, I prayed earnestly, "God, I will not let You go until You bless me. Enlarge my territory. Keep me from harm."

Fifty people were allowed inside the room at any one time. My ticket number was D52. By the time number D38 appeared on the screen, I felt as though I was at Ralph's Supermarket, waiting to buy a pound of ham. Cell phones rang here and there and were answered in languages I did not understand. Faces were stoic, older ones looking either vacant or anxious, while the younger ones had their eyes constantly moving between the booths, the security guards, and the numbers on the screen. The murmur of conversation was subdued. Emotions rustled with the suppressed whispering, only just below the surface. The room smelled of sweat and spices as the fan moved air languidly through the windowless space. By number D39 I was emotionally drained.

I did not like the ropes. I did not like waiting uncertainly, out of control, depending on the good will of someone with whom I had no relationship. It felt like a prison. It was. I was trapped and at their mercy.

I bent my will to adapt to stoicism, patience, and gentle

obsequiousness—matching their eyes, their posture, and their attitude. One misstep and there would be no mercy for me. Two guards stood at the door, apelike, badges agleam on their chests and shoulders. Huge baton-like weapons stood at attention at their sides. Had they ever used them? Would they?

There are times when I have needed to stand very still in this paper bag of life. There is value in being noticed sometimes. Sometimes it is more advantageous to blend, bend, and obey.

IMMIGRATION AGAIN

Twenty-nine of us perch outside.
We sit on the fence,
perch on the grass,
or lean against the wall.
It is warm.
The breeze is light.
Healthy.
Sky is California blue, and clear.
We stand now.
Some inner voice commands the line.
We move as one.
Stand.
Look.
Silent query.
Lean again.
Quiet voices start again.

Tired faces.
Resigned bodies.

A mother carrying her sleeping child
walks past me
down the hill.
Away.
Her husband follows,
papers in hand.
What will be their fate?
What did they learn?
How long the wait?

I was sitting.
Now I stand,
drawing closer
step by step.
It took me thirty minutes to get here.
My work permit card runs out today.
New papers were filed in February.
"He makes all things beautiful
in His time."

Some are allowed
into the hallowed hallways of the INS.
The Immigration and Naturalization Service.
The line moves.
One body.

One purpose.
'Help me!'

Security man. Big-bellied. Black-haired. Young.
Emotionless face.
"Out!
To the rail!
I need your cooperation here!
Move back! Move down!
Away from the door!
Move down!
Come on, move down!
A little cooperation here.
Move away from the door!"

Back we shuffle.
Reluctant.
Resistant.
We want to go forwards.
Any backward step,
is a backward step,
no matter who is giving the orders.
He has a gun.
He has a *nulla nulla.*
A *shillelagh.*
That's what I need.
A shillelagh.
Uncle Eddy had one,

always by his door.
He felt protected.

Security comes again.
A torch too.
Gun,
baton,
torch.
Badges too.
Big badges.
He brings a piece of paper.
Written on it
roughly,
in pencil,
END OF THE LINE.
"Anyone else comes,
  show them this—
  END OF THE LINE."
The sun continues to shine
unperturbed.
The breeze is gentle.
Unflurried.

US ARMY CID
is written
on a sign
outside this room.
Inside now.

WHY WAIT IN LINE? a poster asks.
Why indeed?
Ever tried to garner information
from the INS
via telephone?
Dial.
Answering machine.
Auto redial.
Forty-five minutes.
No human to be found.
Why wait in line?
That's why.

Thirty-four people
in front of me
in line.
Nothing has changed
in two weeks.
Wild black tire marks
still cling
to the otherwise highly polished
white vinyl floor.
Who does what
in here at night?
Some tracks run up the wall.
Do they run under it?
There is mysterious life in the INS
after dark.

"You write too much,"
says the young Mexican man in front of me.
His shirt says, *Banco Ficohsa # 12.*
I shake my head.
Laughter is missing here.
I look for humor
and find it only in the tire marks on the floor.
"I look for Your face, God.
I seek Your face."

Back around the ropes now.
Mr. Security watches
from his chair.
Anxious.
Ready to move.
Keep within the lines.
The rules.
Obey.
Power.
Intimidation.
Ken Medema sings, "Color Outside the Lines."
This
is what I will do.
Color.
Big brush.
Like the purple-cow card I love.
I will write.
I will paint.

Big canvas, big color, big brush.
Simple,
clean,
loud color.
Humor.

Dribbly red stains
are on the floor
near the place my feet have moved to.
Murder here?
At night?
Only fifteen people in front of me now,
in the hallway.

But through the door
in the inner sanctum
I will be able to take a number.
I will be able to sit.
There is a green plant here.
One green plant
in the corner in front of me,
raisin' in the sun.
Except that
there ain't no sun.
This is a death.
A little death.
But not the *petit morte*
of the sexual experience.

This is
death by degrees.
Of self-respect.
Of hope.
Of trust.

"God, show me Your face," I beg.
"Some trust in horses,
 and some trust in chariots,
 but we will trust
'In the name of the Lord Our God,'
 sing the Psalms."

I am next to the plant.
Except that
it is not a plant.
It is a fake.
Of course.
The only sun in here
is in the undaunted human spirit.
Even lights are off.
Of twenty-eight fluorescent lights
five are alight.
Three seats.
All for security men.
Two rubbish bins.
For what?
Four divider screens.

Hiding air?
We wait.
Leaning.
Standing.
Squatting.
We wait.

I will paint
with big
bright
wild colors.
I am ready.
I will write.
I am looking,
and looking.
"Show me Your face."

Laguna Niguel 3:20 p.m.

My file has gone
to an officer.
"What does that mean?"
"It is out of this file.
It is with a woman
in a cubicle."

"How long now?"
"Fifteen days."

"Then?"
Research.
"She will send for the card to be printed."
"The card?"
"The Green Card."

So small.
Representing
so much.
So very much.

"Smile at her please,"
I beg.
"I will try," she said.
No promises.
No commitments.
Not responsible for anything.
I stand
within the ropes.
Inside the lines.

I must be still
and alert.
Steady.
Ready.
Patient.
Inside the lines.
So that

I may,
at the moment of release,
dance,
paint,
write,
sing,
and color
outside the lines.

This is the petit morte.
For a time.
For a season.
But soon,
release,
freedom,
sun,
beach.
A new life
with no ropes,
no boundaries,
except for
the voices of my mind.

Life in my paper bag has never been as I imagined it might be.

A MISSIONARY BY GAD

Auntie Dell owned a mansion of a house in Hawthorne, Victoria, which she turned into a boarding house in order to pay the bills. The common dining room was enormous. From time to time the tables were removed and dozens of extra chairs carried in. Invited friends sat quietly on those chairs as the honored guests walked to the front. One piqued my interest as a child. Garbed in traditional Chinese dress, he walked, moved, and spoke as a Chinese, and yet he was definitely not Chinese. A returned missionary, he was an Australian who had departed our shores to live in China forty years before.

There he had taken on the Chinese manner of living, thinking, speaking, working, and walking. In Auntie Dell's dining room, he attached huge pieces of white paper to an easel and with large, elegant brushes painted symbols using the magic of calligraphy. I copied the symbols for house, Jesus, and heaven, using my pencil and little pad of paper as he told of an exotic life. He so intrigued and impressed me that I came to think that becoming a missionary was a thing to aspire to, and that China was a place to go.

Years later I heard exotic tales told by missionaries who had returned from "darkest Africa." I heard tales of inspiration and of terror, and of diseases with unpronounceable names. And I thought that becoming a missionary was a thing to aspire to, and that possibly Africa was a place to go. Willis would say,

"Wouldn't it be wonderful to have a chance to be a missionary?" In his mind it was the highest of callings. One friend went off to Papua New Guinea as a medical missionary and came back with tales of spirits and spears and wars, and the lives of the people to whom she brought medicine and hope. And I thought that a missionary was a thing to aspire to, and that possibly Papua New Guinea was a place to go. But I did not go. And I was not a missionary.

And then one day I stood next to a person who dressed me down, yelling furiously at me, "We could never have gone to a mission station, because you would never have tolerated all that dirt and mess!" I replied that he had never asked. I guessed that he wanted me to feel his guilt because he had not gone himself. But I still thought a missionary was a thing to aspire to—and a mission station a place to go. But I did not go. Now I did not even want to go. I was not sure how I had missed that calling.

Years passed, and I went to California to work with an author—an entrepreneur and an encourager—to encourage him and to encourage the people he loved and cared for. An Australian friend who came to visit laughingly showed me a photograph I had sent of me standing in front of my favorite Mercedes 420E, framed in front of a gorgeous California sunset. "Jillian," he said, "I have pinned this photo on the notice board of our church in Australia. Underneath is written, 'Our California missionary.'"

I was a missionary? And I didn't even know.

By return mail I sent them another photograph to pin on

their notice board, with me wearing the largest tiara I could find. Across it I wrote, "I won the Miss Missionary World contest, and I got to choose my own crown."

Miss Missionary World

I HAVE TO GO NOW

"In southern California,
people are individualized."

It helped me
that she said that.

I had felt alone.

But she was from Boston.
"It is more pedestrian back east,"
she had said.

I had been continually
astonished
by the lack of community.
"They,
the great amorphous mass,
do not connect,"
I had said.

"But
they are individualized,"
she had said.
It seemed kinder,
truer,
less judgmental.

I love them.
But they
drive me
nuts.

Individualized?

This fact is observed
only

by strangers,
or foreigners,
or aliens.
Like me.

Theirs,
this West Coast group,
is not a dance
with the weaving
in and out
like the Fair Isle patterned knitwear
of the Shetland Islands
of Scotland.
Nor is it
the dance
of the earthquake-ravaged
islands
of New Zealand.

Nor is it in
the rituals
of birthing
and dying,
of love,
and of plighted troth.

Their dance
is in their heads.

Without
the commitment
to love,
honor,
and cherish,
forsaking
all others.
That dance, too,
is individualized.

I have to go.
Now.
To Florida.

"But there are bugs out there,"
they told me.
"Big bugs.
And
it rains!
It rains all the time."

And then,
"It's not so much
the bugs.
It's
the alligators!"

Is that why

I am going
back east,
to Florida?

The bugs,
the rain
and
the alligators?

All are very familiar
to an Australian girl
so far
from home.

Is that why
I feel welcome?
Out there?

REVENGE

My hands glowed with an unearthly orange hue. It had all
begun with a slightly elevated cholesterol level, which led to
Griff hovering. He leaned in close to whisper, "Metamucil.
That's all you need. It is guaranteed to work. It will bring your
cholesterol level right down where it belongs. One teaspoon
each night in your favorite drink." One teaspoon each night in
my favorite drink? Sounded easy. As I couldn't find a trial size,
the container I bought was enormous. It smelled harmless

enough and looked like pale orange jelly crystals. It tasted harmless enough, insipid in fact. Insipid in juice. Insipid in water. Insipid in lemonade. It even tasted insipid in wine. It was so joyless that it made me feel insipid. Because of its stultifying nature I was not mentally inspired to remember the one-teaspoon-in-a-drink routine.

In order to facilitate a better use of my memory for the purpose of taking Metamucil, I decanted it into a glass container, which sat pertly on the kitchen bench and disturbed my carefully planned décor. It disturbed me too. I thrust it into the refrigerator in a half-hearted attempt to keep it full of vim and vigor.

Some months after Griff's well-meaning advice, I was preparing to move house and sorting through kitchen items—and there it was again, glaring at me balefully from the depths of the refrigerator, imprisoned like the turkey. Metamucil glared at me from the refrigerator? It had taken on a life of its own.

Frantic with guilty courage I moved in to deal with it, and into the garbage disposal went the whole lot. My cholesterol level was lowered instantly by the aggressive act of tossing it into oblivion, loudly proclaiming, "Farewell!" Hot water gushed from the faucet and I ran the disposal. O joy! Until, faster than the speed of light, sickly-looking sweet-smelling Metamucil gloop stunned the garbage disposal into immovability. How that stuff moves through anyone's system remains a mystery to me. It did not like that I had avoided my nightly dose. It did not like that I had left it abandoned, imprisoned, and trapped in isolation in the refrigerator. I caught the hint of

a ghoulish orange leer from the depths of the disposal, treach-
erously bogged up, stopped-up, stuck, and immovable. I had
no choice but to dive in and clean the whole lot out. I was left
with luminous orange hands.

Orange gloop had caught me in Metamucil revenge.

I did not ever imagine that my paper bag of life would
pick me up one more time and wing me back to Melbourne
town, to love and marry for as long as we both should live.
Melbourne, Vancouver, Chicago, Sydney, Chicago, Beverly
Farms, Salem, Providence, Fall River, Sydney, California—and
then Melbourne again. It was enough to make a girl beg for
the paper bag to stop opening and closing. And I thought that
my life would be ordinary?

But my rellies moved around and about this globe too.
Perhaps it is a genetic trait I inherited to prepare me
for my own paper bag of life.

THE BOX

They lie
as if in state,
in a box.
In yellow files,
paper and words
carry forward
their hopes and their dreams.

To a sunburned land they came.
James,
my paternal great-grandfather,
from Devonshire,
England,
in 1843.
What hopes? What dreams?

Mary,
my paternal great-grandmother,
from county Tyrone,
Ireland,
sailed on the Frankfield.
Nineteen hundred tons
with 302 souls on board
they say.
Occupation: housemaid.
Religion: Protestant.
Literate.
The government paid
nineteen pounds towards her passage.

One male adult,
three male children
and four female children
died on that journey.
Four births were recorded.

Married they were,
Mary and James,
at the parish of Saint James,
Melbourne.

Of this union
George was born,
in Collingwood, Victoria,
in 1846.

George married Mary Anne.
He was twenty-six,
she, seventeen.

But died he did, aged forty-one,
from head injuries
sustained in a fall
from a horse.
And she was left,
with eight children
aged from fifteen years
to one.

The fourth child,
Ada Elizabeth,
only nine years old
at the time,
became my paternal grandmother.

LIFE IN A PAPER BAG

Ada Elizabeth married
Edward Dewar Richards,
of Boweya North, Victoria,
July 11, 1900,
on her twenty-first birthday.

And somewhere in there lies
Buck Richards, who fought on the southern side in the
American Civil War, when he passed through the US on his
way to New Zealand.
He fought in the Fifty-fifth Mc Coins (Tennessee) Infantry, or
the Twentieth Mississippi Regiment Volunteers. Or both. Or
so they say.

I always liked the sound of
Buck.

Alongside these
in the box,
lie Antonio and Agnes.
He from Balletta,
northeast of Naples,
Italy,
and later of the Greek island
of Corfu.

He sailed to
the Port of Geelong, Victoria,

on a ship
of which his brother
Michael
was the captain.

Jumped ship he did,
and headed
for the goldfields.
Walking.
He walked on and on,
from Creswick
to Jump-Up
and on and on,
to Ballarat,
to take part
in the Eureka Stockade
of 1854.

Agnes
was born at Lochmaben,
County of Dumfries,
Scotland
in 1837.

Sailed she did,
at the age of two,
aboard the Lady Lilford
to Port Adelaide, South Australia.

Antonio and Agnes
met in Creswick, Victoria,
and married on June 28, 1856.

She was nineteen,
he, thirty-nine.

Eight children
she bore him,
and died,
aged thirty-six.

Antonio married again,
and died,
aged ninety-seven.

These were my
maternal great-grandparents.

The box
contains them:
my forbears.
The yellow files
contain them.

But
they are not contained,
and

they are not confined.

For I am
bone of their bone,
and flesh of their flesh,
a living product
of their hopes and their dreams.

BUCK RICHARDS

They say that my great-great uncle sailed to the US to fight in the Civil War. This could solve the family mystery concerning the name Buck. I have one photograph of him only, the rest is conjecture.

"I have to leave this London town,
it's cold and grey and dark.
I have to leave this London town
to make a whole new start.
There is a place for me to own,
I feel it in my heart."

So he sailed far away
on a fine midsummer's day,
sailed
from the English Port of Devon.
He hastened on his way
to the new US of A,

his belly full of fire,
or so they say.

He sailed for many a day
to the land of USA,
a land where they said
he could make his way.
"This land," he mused each day,
"might just be heaven."

But the air was filled with lead
and he bowed down his head,
while they counted up their dead.
It was not heaven.

What he saw burned in his heart
and he didn't want a part
of the endless, endless,
endless, endless talking.
For, "What's the use,
what's the use,
of talking?"

"Put me here by your side
In this anguished field of battle.
Let me fight, let me fight
'til we've won.

"Let me fight for my manhood,
Let me fight with you, friend.
We will fight
For a world well worth saving."

"We will ride it together
this great stallion of fear,
ride it for all that we see.
This land if truly free,
could just be heaven."

"But what's the use of talking
when a man cannot be free?
what's the use,
what's the use of talking?"

They called this tall man
Buck,
a name that now has stuck,
to a tall man,
a lean man,
a hard man,
a mean man,
Buck Richards.

Frontier men
fighting war.
Civil War,

what's the score?
Fighting mad
their spirits soar,
as bullets roar.
"I can't do more,"
Buck Richards.

RICHARDS'

I wish I had been smart enough to keep a diary with the title, *Family Richards*. It took me a while to understand that families can have a commercial value if observed with a jaundiced eye, and all doings good bad or awful noted in a secret place. I talk about *them* in parenthesis, as though I am separate from their eccentric, irreverent, and occasionally wickedly funny world. Each of the ones I knew exhibited their eccentricity gladly and I continue to be drawn to the zanier people I meet.

NOT EIGHTY

In exactly fourteen days he would roll up his saddlebag for the very last time and depart this mortal coil. The steps at the front of 54 Wheatland Road, Malvern where he fell were neither steep nor many. Other elderly mourners trod with care as they followed in the footsteps of friends and family, holding an arm here or a hand there to comfort and guide. He did not remember his fall and could not answer those who moved toward his side with concern, to ask what happened. He remembered only being fleet of foot as a youth. It was not easy to remember the more recent days; they slid from his grasp or sat silent at the edges of his mind as his thoughts brushed past them, searching. How many times he had loped his way down those very same steps to sit in the sun on the lower ones. How many times he had gathered his coat around his loins, defending himself against the rain or the blasting wind. He knew the sound of his feet on each step. In the slather of wet or in the quiet of the night, in the cool of early morning or of early dawn he knew them. But today he had missed a step, and although he was as mad as hell, he sure was not going to tell them how he felt. Let them guess.

Why had they all come here to disturb his life, tossing their idle conversation across his path? They had huddled together and hovered around the tables laden with food like a pack of jackals. And where was Ada when he needed her? The chalky hip that shattered when he fell caused enough anguish to penetrate his soul. It hurt in places that did not expect injury. He swallowed a little, trying to move the spittle in his mouth to a more comfortable place. His body would not settle itself, and his soul felt undone and trapped all at the same time. He was all bent out of shape. And where was Ada when he needed her?

All this I saw as a ten-year-old sees, through uncomprehending eyes. I was surrounded by emotions that I did not recognize and for which I had no names. I could see but not interpret. He was my paternal grandfather, Edward Dewar Richards, grey-haired and grumpy. Neighbors, family, and friends had gathered at the Richards's family home for the funeral of his wife, my paternal grandmother, Ada Elizabeth Dennis Richards.

In a photograph taken of them on their wedding day they were about as handsome a pair as set sail for a life of wedded bliss. Ada Elizabeth wore a pin-tucked dress of white silk, which demurely covered every provocative curve of her female anatomy. At her neck, a brooch fashioned from two bars of gold was decorated with pearls and diamonds. The lace on her dress ruffled its way right up to her chin, lest any bold man should chance to think there was a real live woman within. Her hands gentled a bashful bouquet of Cecil Brunner roses and Lily of the Valley. She did not smile. Edward Dewar stood arrogantly, decked out in a snappy black suit, displaying the bushy moustache known at the turn of the century for its ability to attract the fairer sex.

It was Ada Elizabeth's twenty-first birthday the day they were married in the year 1900. And now this day, as their progeny gathered along with a lone piper to farewell Ada Elizabeth, it was all far past Edward Dewar's comprehension. There had not been enough man in him to make it with grace to the bottom of the steps. He fell and he did not want their help, those fussing kids of his. He did not want to meet their eyes, not a single one of them.

I do not remember much of Edward Dewar, but from time to time tales of him were told over family repasts of the birthday, Christmas, or Easter kind. With bellies full, family stories were brought out to share time and again. "A barnyard rooster," I heard, once. I did not know what in the world that could possibly mean. "He played the violin," Anne Miree had whispered to me, despite the fact that neither of us had ever seen that. "He played at the Malvern Town Hall every Saturday night. Don't you remember seeing him coming in through the front door with his violin case, wearing evening dress?" I did not. Later I would discover the truth, which was that Edward Dewar was a Mason, coming home in evening dress and carrying his little black bag of tricks. The family was so dismayed by this fact that it was not spoken of in my presence.

There was no regalia on this day though, except that which was worn by the lone piper. Edward Dewar looked pale and limp, wrinkled and lost like a forgotten rag doll as he lay at the bottom of the steps. He had sat at the head of the table at family gatherings over many years. Maids fussed and squabbled in the kitchen while we paid court to him in a courteous but not very connected way. There was a marvelous eccentricity about my relatives, and stories of "the farm" abounded. There were stories of the shilling that Edward Dewar handed out to his teenage sons at the end of each backbreaking week of work. With this meager allowance they transported themselves by means of a dray to the local dance at Bowyer North, or to the Almonds, or to St. James, where the already notorious Kelly family were known for their hair-raising exploits. Edward Dewar listened to their banter, always appearing disconnected.

Entertainment on the farm had taken the form of Edward Dewar sitting on the long front porch in the evening playing the piccolo like a dirge. "That was it," said Willis, "that was our only entertainment." One by one the kids left the the farm and

"the old man" and his smithy business by the St. James railway
station and headed for the city of Melbourne to try their luck.
Their share of the farm would come to them in the old man's
good time, but they were not prepared to wait. Despite all the
family camaraderie and banter, I never once heard Edward
Dewar speak. As far as I knew he never had.

"The farm." When I finally visited after so many years of
Willis's stories, I came back, all excited to tell him. "Now you
can see why I left," he said. I was flummoxed!

A year or two before Ada Elizabeth's funeral we had sat
cheek to jowl at the laden kitchen table, gathered together to
share in the celebration of Edward Dewar's eightieth birthday.
The children—having turned cartwheels on the lawn, explored
the bluestone lane behind the house, crept up the dimly lit
hallway with its green velvet curtains, investigated the ancient
outside toilets with their long wooden seats, counted the number of marble fireplaces, and kept cricket balls from shattering
the stained glass windows—finally settled into their seats.

We sat at the feast fit for the man of the hour. The "boys"
joked and yarned about their dad as we jostled for attention

amidst much good-humored laughter. Grandfather was eighty, and barnyard rooster or not, he had made quite a mark on the world. His life was worth celebrating. As he sat at the head of the table and watched us, not a muscle of his face moved, only his eyes. He did not nod in assent or scowl in disagreement. He just sat. As the last farm story ebbed away into silence— Uncle Eddie, as the eldest, made a little speech and offered a toast to their father on his eightieth. We readied ourselves to stand.

Until Edward Dewar Richards cleared his throat. He slowly cast his faded blue eyes the length and breadth of the table, surveying his clutch, his mob, his tribe, his kids. The silence was instant and heart-stoppingly loud. "I am not eighty," he intoned. "I am seventy-nine."

NAMING A STONE

Uncle Eddie loved fiddling around in his shed and fossicking at the dump. Occasionally duty called him to return to holding the Australian nation to account in his role as Chief of Federal Police, until what he called "the iron in my blood," called him back to his shed. He was also known to offer gifts of beautiful, colored, river stones that he had found, polished, and set. As I too love beautiful stones, I consider this to be a genetic quality, inherited directly from Eddie.

When I visited the historic town of Tombstone in Arizona the streets were swarming with folk dressed in exotic Western dress who had roared into town on their Harley Davidsons, wearing slick Stetsons and carrying side-arms. Other folk had rolled into town in their old pick-up trucks, wearing battered Stetsons, and also carrying sidearms. A slew of fabulously dressed paid performers were there also, providing the feel of authenticity in the endless promenade up and down the main street. We all joined in our love for Tombstone's colorful past, but it was difficult to tell what was real and what was fantastic in Tombstone.

I carried no sidearms, but I did carry a strong desire to purchase something wonderful as a reminder of Tombstone. After a full day of searching I finally stood before the owner of a jewelry store explaining that I was looking for the spectacular. Not satisfied with the jewelry on display, I pointed to the back of her store. "You must have something spectacular out there," I said, hoping not to leave empty-handed. She nodded knowingly and returned with a heavy-set piece of Tombstone joy in her hand. Set in silver, the stone was spectacular. Each time I have returned to Tombstone I have been stopped on the street by some craggy-faced old miner who wants to know where I purchased such a very old stone, and how long I have owned it.

"We haven't mined that stuff for years. It's a beauty," I have heard again and again as they grin their pleasure.

Today, I cannot remember the name of that stone, and it is driving me crazy. I am reminded of Uncle Eddie. "Sometimes, when I go out to the garage," he told me in his later years," I cannot remember what it was I came out for. So I start going through the alphabet. A, B, C ...." Here he paused to check my face to see if I was taking him seriously. "But the trouble is that after a while I stand there thinking—why am I going through the alphabet?" We laughed.

But today I am not laughing much. I cannot for the life of me remember the name of the stone in my treasured piece of Tombstone jewelry, and I have tried the alphabet, and I do remember why it is that I am going through it. A whole afternoon has passed and the file has not raised itself from its slumber in my head. So I try again.

A.

Amber: I have a fabulous piece of that which I bought for 70 percent off and love to this day.

Amethyst: Griff gave me a huge piece and surprised me speechless one Christmas.

Ammonite: I was entranced once by a huge exotic-looking shell in a Vancouver window. It was the most fabulously iridescent thing I had ever seen, and love at first sight. It held out its arms to me, begging. In answer to my inquiry concerning the price, I thought I heard $3,200. "Very rare," the proprietor told me. "The mine is running out." I winced in pain. How wrong I was. The price was $32,000. I howled.

B.

Beryl is the first gem that comes to mind. And beads of course, but not much value there.

C.

Citrine. Mr. T gave me an elegant citrine Art Deco ring he bought as a Paris memory for me. I love it.

D.

Well, diamonds—they say—are a girl's best friend.

E.

Emeralds. Lovely things, but I do not have any of those.

Ebony. Beautiful stuff, but not a stone.

F.

What in the world could I put here? Furniture comes to mind. No good. Figs? Fur? Now there is something every girl who had ever been in Sweden or Chicago in winter needs, but it is not close to the stone department.

G.

Gold. Warm glowing stuff. The Incas and the Pre-Incas made huge items of headwear and earrings from gold and carried their leaders on their shoulders through the streets of their cities—a glowing, gorgeous and revered lot.

H.

Heartfelt thanks for what I have is all I can think of. Helium? Health? That's the jewel here.

I.

Ink. To write love letters. They could be jewels.

K.

Kryptonite. Superman stuff.

L.

Lapis. Lovely blue. I gave some to my daughter-in-law. I hope she still has it.

M.

Marble. Makes me think of death.

N.

Nuts. Sweet healthy food. I am warm with the thought of them.

O.

Opals of course. Beautiful Australian stones.

P.

And then there are pearls.

Q.

Not even my imagination can conjure up a stone here. Although quince when cooked into a jelly is jewel-like and delicious.

R.

Rubies are warm-sounding and gentle. Everyone I knew as a child had a Ruby somewhere in their family. Great aunts, or neighbors, or your mother's best friend had this name. They never seemed to be anything but big-bosomed, good-hearted folk.

S.

Silver. So much of it in so many stores but you have to search to find it finely wrought. Much is stored in my cupboards and none of my children want anything to do with it. I have taken loads to the thrift shop. Seashells, too, are fine things, but they are not my stone.

T.

I want to say Titanium. Light. Useful. Amazing. But not my stone either.

U.

I am about to say umbrella, because I am getting tired, and tired of the whole exercise.

V.

Violets here, because Auntie Dell always wore them. And

because, when I was young and gay, you could always buy a bunch here or there in Melbourne town, and they were a thing to bring joy.

W.

Where will I go if I cannot bring this stone into my mind? It will have to be Google, and that is a daunting thought. Will this become the only alternative to my brain in a year or two from now? Instead of not remembering why I went out to the garage, I may well not remember why I have turned to Google.

X.

Xanadu…wherever that may be.

Y.

Young faces. These are the jewels.

Z.

Zis iz zee end. Google it has to be. Oh, rats!

Commissioner Edward Richards.

WILLIS

Willis was eccentric in many ways. The windows of our home at 45-B Bowen Street were covered in the wooden venetian blinds that were considered a luxury after the Second World War, but ended up so far past their prime that they needed renovation and rejuvenation. Most of all they needed throwing out, but Willis grew up on the farm, where nothing was ever thrown out. Ever. Each year, as spring approached Willis took the venetian blinds down from their moorings and separated the wooden slats from the fiddly tapes that held them together. He hammered up military style rows of nails on his garage wall, patiently painted the top side of each slat with a hand brush, waited for it to dry, turned, painted and dried again, repeating the process laboriously until each side of each slat was returned to its pristine glory, resting to recover on the nails that were drawn up in formation like troops. But once returned inside the house the venetian blinds were expected to have reverent, mind-numbing dusting. I was far from enamored when it was my turn to dust, slat by never-ending slat. Those venetian blinds, the look, the feel, and the daily closing of them as the sun went down, required their own reveille.

But it was not only the multitude of soldierly slats that received the Willis's loving attention; it was the tapes that held the whole kit and caboodle together. These were removed from the slats, washed by hand in warm water and Rinso, hung to dry, and ironed to perfection before being threaded back onto the newly painted slats, a salute to the determination of his undaunted spirit. A product of the Depression, the Second World War, and—most of all—the farm, Willis kept everything for the inevitable day when a use would be found for it.

Forty-five-B? There is even a story about our street number. After the war, Willis was able to purchase not one, but two, blocks of land, adjoining. He was proud that he was able to do that for the family. The blocks were long and thin, and Willis—not satisfied to build on such skinny blocks of land—prevailed upon the reluctant city council to change the configuration in order that they might be divided the opposite way, thus producing wider blocks. The numbers did not quite work out however, hence our 45-B—with the block next door becoming 45-A. With 45-A sold, our 45-B was totally paid for. I think this took all of Willis's enterprising energy, as he remained as fiscally conservative as any I have known, and it remained his wont to pay cash for all things—land, houses, or cars. Anything.

A metal spike, impaled unceremoniously into a small, highly polished piece of wood and kept on the top shelf of the food cupboard in our kitchen, served as Willis's filing system. Incoming bills were paid immediately—the receipts impaled on the metal spike for the remainder of their days.

In the garage a ball of rubber bands settled dustily into place beside a box of string—smelling ancient, feeling glutinous, ominously dark, and too big to hold easily in the hand. For what purpose were these kept? I never knew, and now I will never know. Willis died before I had the temerity to ask. I have not been able to keep even one rubber band in my home office since.

Then there were tools. Layer upon dusty layer of tools. The garage, which was so very tidy and orderly at a cursory glance, kept very quiet about its secrets. Willis eventually forgot about the first layer of tools he had brought with him from 'the farm. They were the very expensive, heavy, last-a-lifetime kind of tools. As he moved into another part of his life and mind, he purchased a second set, and a third set, and even a fourth set, of everything. By the end of his life he had discovered the joy of the two-dollar shop. And there he bought tools for which he had no purpose, simply for the joy of buying a tool of any kind for two dollars. He never did get over this pleasure.

When he died there were many things to deal with. There was a two-foot length of chain, too heavy to lift; a milking bucket from the farm he had left sixty years before, and rows of extra wooden venetian blind slats, seated primly on their nails.

As he aged and became seriously eccentric, Willis would occasionally rail about the war and yell, "You would have been a waitress in a Japanese restaurant if it was not for me!" But cheap Japanese goods came to be okay, simply because they were so cheap. And eventually Chinese goods came to be okay too, simply because they were so cheap.

Following Willis's death, my older son, Luke Benjamin, decided he would make order of the garage and its contents. After twenty-four hours of patient categorizing and the making of endless heaps of "stuff," he was pummeled into frothing, slathering submission. We ordered a skip. Then? We ordered another.

45b Bowen Street

STRING

When Willis died there was a lot to do.

The boy had left the farm, but the farm had never quite left the boy.

He was a funny man. Eccentric even. The last time I saw him alive he came out to greet me wearing a pair of terrible short-shorts and a ratty old Australian hat all tied around with corks, which bobbed their fantastic dance on little strings. The ugly, dark-blue, cotton hat was floppy in the Australian way. I had never seen it before. Where in the world could he have found such a thing? The corks and their strings carried the definite look of Willis's handiwork. A pale-blue, sadly bedraggled cardigan topped the shorts and shirt, a dismal nod to propriety. And in his mouth? A huge pink pacifier. His grin was wicked, his blue eyes agleam with his joy at all this nonsense. If it were not true, I would have told you, but I have a photograph to prove it. He knew his time was short, and we were not going to be sad. Who else's father would do such a thing?

A lover of all things Australian, Willis had never left the bush behind. The corks were a nod to the swagmen who had tramped the road to Yarrawonga where Willis and his family farmed. The corks kept the Aussie flies at bay. He loved the swagmen's fortitude and their ballads. He also loved the old Indian trader who brought goods to the back door of the family home and was fed a nourishing meal by my grandmother every time he came. Willis's spirit was generous in that same Richards way.

I grew up with Willis perched on the end of my bed regaling me with stories of the farm. When I finally made my own pilgrimage to the farm with my young children, I came back to tell Willis. His response? "Now you can see why I left." The cad! But he never really did, not in his spirit.

Willis loved Australian literature and poetry. *A Fortunate Life* by A. B. Facey was a favorite. "Could have been my story," he said. And it could. He loved Banjo Patterson. His own poetry trudged to the rhythm of the Australian landscape. "These boots are made for walking," he wrote in his own poems about the Australian bushmen.

He determined that this Australian girl needed practical training to fit her for life. "Mallee roots," he said, "are the only things to burn on an open fire. Nothing burns like them. Let me show you how to split a Mallee root." And he did. No shirking for this Australian girl. Not under Willis's tutelage. It tickles my fancy that a Mallee Root festival is held annually in

Ouyen and that it includes a Mallee Root Toss, in which folk of all ages can compete. I cannot imagine why Willis did not drag us all there. Perhaps Merle was not keen. The next Mallee Root Festival is in my diary patiently waiting for COVID-19 to pass. "Let me show you how to sharpen an axe," said Willis. And he did. "Let me show you how to drop a bore." And he did. "Let me show you how to prime the pump." And he did. "Let me show you how to syphon petrol from a gas tank." I hated the smell of the rubber hose and the taste of the petrol, and I

The last time I saw Willis. Dressed in his "best" so I would not be sad.

forgot to ask why in the world I might need this skill. Was this for a little covert stealing?

But he was gone now. Stone cold dead in his bed with his clothes on. No retirement home for Willis. No nursing home for him. "They will carry me out of here in a box," he said. And they did. Stubborn he was too. Generous. Gregarious. Funny. Neighborly. And a religious fanatic. A bundle of contradictions, he was at his best with his siblings or comrades from the Second World War, giggling the Richards giggle—or quietly remembering Singapore, Morotai, Balikpapan. And he was at his worst when his self-righteous bigotry took over in the church, which was never rigidly fundamentalist enough for him. Then he was both rigid and cantankerous.

But he was gone now. Stone cold dead. And there was a lot to do.

Ultimately it was the garage, (originally a fibro-cement shed, and then with enough cash saved, a double garage built of clinker bricks to match the house), that nearly did us all in. "Clinker bricks," said Willis, "are the only bricks to use, ever. They are double fired. See these marks. This is how you can tell they are true clinker. They are somewhat burned in the second firing. Strong as iron they are." His clinker brick garage became his safe house. His fortitude builder. His place to tinker and to work. His place to pat his new FJ Holden reverently and whisper sweet nothings to her. "Nothing ever went up a hill like this," he would say. "Don't even have to change gears. Look at this."

Under the hood, silent as death, a police siren waited until

Willis's desire to terrify some poor unsuspecting soul into kingdom come overcame him. Where did he get it? I have my suspicions but will never say, although his brother was Chief Commissioner of Federal Police for twenty years. Even met the Queen he did. But that is a story for another time.

And now, with Willis's departure the clinker brick garage stood silent, apparently neat and well organized. "I'll do it, Mum," said Luke and started into the big sort. By midnight he appeared at the door looking like an apparition from the depths of the Scottish coalmines. Blackened from head to toe and standing beside a pile of things to go to the dump that reached past his shoulder in height and covered square meters of floor space, he reluctantly admitted defeat. "Too much for me," he said with a grin. And still the garage looked untouched. "There are layers, Mum. Layers and layers!" The garage, it seemed, was in fact a true geological site. Layer upon layer of Willis's life was revealed as we worked our way back to life on the farm at St. James, which Willis had left at the age of seventeen.

Willis forgot that he already had one of this or that tool, one or two of everything. One or two of this or that. Jars of nails, tacks, screws, light globes, old matches, rubber bands, and string. We found a milking bucket. From the farm. We found a tin full of tacks and leather soles ready for shoe repair. From my school days. We found a short length of chain almost too heavy to lift. From the farm. We found every tool a man could ever need in this life or the next. "On the farm," said Willis, "we did not throw anything away."

We found a parcel wrapped in thick brown paper and tied with string. It revealed itself as a beautiful dress I had worn twenty years prior as a bridesmaid for my best friend. We found my very first bedspread. We found money. Quite a bit. We found details of his fifteen years of research into the family tree, and we found multitudes of expensive German tools that were covered over entirely by cheaper tools from the two-dollar shops which now commanded Willis's attention.

We hired a dumpster. We called friends and distant relatives who came and went with sly grins and trailers bulging, until finally and triumphantly filthy from the doing of it, we found one last gift of Willis joy. A box was unearthed, measuring in length and width the size of a large shoebox. It had found its way to the surface, reluctantly. What new delight could this be? More cash? Maybe a gold bar. But there it was, another eccentric Willis triumph. Collected with fastidious care and grinning up at us from the inside of the box were myriad pieces of string. String! Old string too, and grimy with years of garage dust. A box full of it. String! But the pleasure of it all was right with us to the very last breath. Staring right into our eyes from the side of the box were the bold words only Willis would dare to write. STRING TOO SHORT TO USE. I could hear Willis giggle. I am sure of it. String too short to use?

It was.

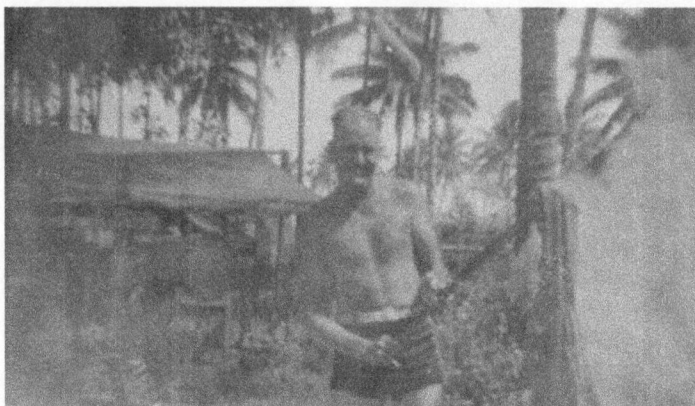

Willis on washing day.

GRIM REAPER

Gladys was the only girl in a family with five boys. Gladys would have made a good boy, but then, she made a good girl too. She could never bring herself to leave the country. The four boys left Grandpa Richards to his farm and his measly one shilling a week and went off to the city. They never returned to country living but talked of it endlessly for the rest of their lives. George became an accountant; Edward, the Chief of Federal police; Willis, an Air Force officer; and Percy, a chemist. City life was for them, but not for Gladys. From St. James she made her way to the Victorian country town of Kyabram, where she lived for the remainder of her life.

The four brothers adored Gladys, and she them. She rode horses. She baked the world's best fruitcake. She taught her dog to sing. She grew the sweetest tomatoes and bottled them. She became a scout leader, and would holler out her "DYB,

DYB, DYB. Do your best. Do your best. Do your best." To which we would holler back, "DOB, DOB, DOB. Do our best. Do our best. Do our best." Her scones won every blue ribbon in the country shows and the cream she lavished on them tasted like the breath of cows.

Clan Richards' events were always mirth-filled, with much high-pitched girlish giggling at their own jokes to be heard in every corner of Grandpa Richards's house when they gathered for family celebrations. Gladys would hang onto the closest arm, doubled over in ecstasy.

Percy, the youngest, died of a heart attack at fifty, and as his life came to an abrupt stop, so did the giggling for a while. Gladys and the boys were stricken. But by then a devastating stroke had stolen the loquacious Gladys's capacity for speech, except for the one word with which she endeavored to express her torment. "Willis. Willis. Willis," she would say. She could not say Percy's name.

Death tantalized with its "the door is shut in your face" attitude. Nothing was left behind for a hug or a longing look. You were here, and now you are not.

The scene changes constantly in the paper bag of life.

LATIN LESSONS AND FOOTBALL

Sunday roast after church was a ritual at 45-B. The baking tray laden with potatoes and onions, pumpkin and carrots, and groaning with the best cut we could afford, leaked mouth-watering aromas. As we children rushed in from church, we dropped our angelic Sunday morning performance right at the back door.

I wonder who it was who induced Gladys to drape on this tree.

I was a skinny child, in a "not quite grown into her body" kind of way—and always hungry. As Willis carved the Sunday roast, I hovered, dripping desire. He sliced slivers of meat and passed tiny portions to me, balanced reverently on the end of his carving fork. Then he sighed over my skinniness and offered me morsels of fat. "You need this to put a bit of fat on your bones," he would say. I did not like the fat, but the meat I relished. I remember his love.

Weekdays were altogether another scene. We neighborhood kids were all friends, boys with girls, and those who rode new bicycles with those who rode old bicycles. We walked or rode to school, not a parent to be seen. In the evenings it was our wont to play together in the streets until it was either too cold or too dark to stay outside. There I learned the rudiments of Aussie Rules football, including how to manage a dropkick and how to bounce the egg-shaped ball so that it returned to me and did not dance maddeningly away—important skills for any Melbourne girl. I remember camaraderie.

Weekdays during my early high school years wash up feelings of a different hue, and of lessons much harder to learn. They attach caboose-like, to my memories of Sunday roast in Melbourne town.

Toby John is now resident in Gothenburg, Sweden. He is so fluent in the Swedish language that the natives think that perhaps he comes from a different city. No such gift for languages was or is mine, possibly because Melbourne school kids in those years spent endless hours shivering in poorly heated classrooms. Our Latin teacher looked like a relative of the Galapagos tortoise. His hair was greasy and unkempt, as was his suit, which was grey and baggy, and lurched loosely down at the pockets. His tie was permanently askew. His shirt never once gleamed Rinso white. I suffered under him. We all did. I still smart when my mind claps its eyes onto the reddened legs of the boys standing benighted on the wooden seats of their desks, tormented to the point of tears from pain and humiliation. Punishment for the inability to conjugate a Latin verb would be metered out by means of a merciless whack behind the knees with the hard-covered, green, Latin text. The wheals would stand out proud, for hours, sometimes for days. The boys trembled there, mute. I remember terror.

The girls took their punishment in the form of a whack to the head with the same hard-covered, green, Latin text. All Willis's offerings of carved Sunday roast could not protect me from the unleashed fury of this master of Latin who dared to call himself a man. Most of us suffered in silence. There was no advocate. We did not tell our parents or other teachers. We simply held in the pain as well as we could and steeled ourselves for the next onslaught. After school we played Aussie Rules out on the street. I remember camaraderie.

OLD-TIME RELIGION

One more time I landed at the Melbourne airport, returned to Australia after six delightfully frenetic years working in and out of southern California and traveling the length and breadth of the US in the process of what was both an exhilarating and exhausting learning curve. I breathed in the Australia I had left years before. Like a newly hatched chicken shaking out its feathers and finding its way on scratchy little legs, I carefully poked my way back into my next new world of Melbourne town, and as I did, the Australian media bombarded me with a little world news and a lot of football news. Daily, relentlessly, the talk went on and on and on. The talk was so much about Aussie Rules football that I felt bombarded, colliding with this talk hour after hour as I moved through my paces. And then, in the midst of all the football frenzy, there he was, smack bang in the middle of my living room, although try as I might I could not see him at all. At first, I was not sure I could hear him either, there were so many strident male voices vying for my attention. Despite the hiddenness of him, there was something about his quietly resolute nature that thrust its way right through the cacophony of radio voices. He absolutely made my morning.

Up until that moment I had been occupied with the cleaning and sorting of certain peripheral parts of my life. In a very few weeks dust had feathered my new nest when I was not looking, and the angle of the sun glancing in across the cedar venetian blinds startled me into a search for rubber gloves and the willingness to work. The Grundig stereo 4295 German radio poured soothing music over my soul, and I was lulled into the calm determination to pack all particles of dust on their way to dust-heaven.

But nothing lasts forever they say, and somewhere in bowels of the ABC, a decision had been taken to end the music and begin talk of sport. Not just sport. Football. Such was the abrupt and startling change that it frisbeed me from my endeavors into a brand-new orbit. As sharp and confronting as the music had been gentle and comforting, the ABC's football discussion roused me to my feet and then onto a chair in order to reposition my mind. The heated discussion and staggeringly biased comments centered hotly on The Grand Final. Events of September 11, 2001 in faraway New York City had faded into oblivion with the passion of it all. Kings and potentates could scheme and plan at will, but in this city of Melbourne, in this state of Victoria, in this country of Australia, on this particular day, it was all about the Brisbane versus Collingwood game. It was all about Footy. Football. The Grand Final was about to run the nation. Aussie Rules ruled.

On the Grundig radio, hearts were bared, best guesses were offered, and hopeless dreams were expressed. Credit was both given and taken as maudlin memories were resurrected and revisited, turned over and touched with gnarled but gentle hands. Deep feelings expressed as in a confessional, threw their lengthy shadows and occasional spurts of light over my imagination. Up until now my morning had been mundane. But the particular gentleman who spoke through clenched teeth riveted me to the spot with the joy in his voice and the depth of his feelings. His passion was not controlled. He was the one who told me the way it really was, and he made it clear that the way it really was—was the way it should be. Like a veteran returned from a misunderstood war, he tore away any pretense at mediocrity. "I told them years ago!" he boomed. "I told them that the game was in danger of becoming a sport! A sport!! Like any other sport!" He paused and sighed soulfully. "It used to be a religion," he intoned sadly, his voice trembling with melancholy reverence. "It's all changed."

Dust fairies competed with sporting demons, until once more I was bolted unceremoniously back to reality by the announcer telling me that, "Meanwhile, Collingwood supporters have left their hotel to march to the Melbourne Cricket Ground, led appropriately by a lone piper." The last time I had heard a lone piper was at Uncle Eddie's funeral. It was cold then too. Bitter. It was bitterly cold out there on this day in the world of big brave men who were ready to battle it out for the glory of their club, and for the telling of tall tales. This particular bitter cold had caused the Collingwood supporters to be hopelessly, grovelingly grateful. "The temperature is set to top out at 11.3 degrees centigrade. O heaven bless us! It topped out at 11.3 degrees centigrade forty-four years ago, and Collingwood won. Against all odds. Collingwood won! Now that has to be a good omen. The football gods must be smiling."

Bronzed golden from life under the Australian sun in far northern Queensland, the Brisbaners may be made to shrink into oblivion under the vengeful eye of the Melbourne weather gods. If Collingwood won, my passionate radio friend would need to simmer in anguish soup no more. He had told me that Aussie Rules was a religion. Worshipped. Adored. Honored. Sacrificed to. Sacrificed for. Speak quietly. Speak reverently. Shoes off. Tread gently. This could be holy ground.

A few days later I heard that voice again. In the shadow of the MCG, with the pain and tragedy of a humiliating defeat in Collingwood hearts, and exuberant litter outside the Sporting Globe Pub at the end of our street, Collingwood supporters were still groaning with grief and disbelief. "I told them years ago," he had boomed. "I told them that the game was in danger of becoming a sport. Like all other sports!!" And then he paused and sighed soulfully, his voice trembling with melancholy reverence. "It used to be a religion."

The cacophony of noise from the devastating traumas of our present world faded a little as I thought of all that is aggressive and proud and exciting when disciplined athletes gave their minds, hearts, and bodies to the religion that is sport, offering the endless hope of possibilities in the face of defeat and in the face of triumph.

And I tread gently. This could be holy ground.

ESSENDON TOOTHBRUSH

"Scraggly women? Did you say scraggly women? What on earth do you mean?" "Oh, you know," he replied, vexed, "they are scraggly. They don't do anything to themselves. No makeup. Don't do anything to their hair. Scraggly," he finished, underlining that word with his voice. "Anyway, Sandy is all excited about the football. She talked about it nonstop. She thinks it is the most exciting week of the year. 'The Doggies! The Doggies!' she yells. 'The Grand Final!' She is ecstatic."

"Oh yes, the Grand Final," I thought. The Grand Final week has given me cause to smile for many a year now. Although I did grow up in Melbourne town, as a child I was not offered the opportunity to go to a football game, let alone a Grand Final. By the time I returned to live in Melbourne after decades of absence, I thought it high time I gave football a go.

Bob was roped in to help me with the purchase of tickets. He had been a bit of a local football star in his youth, and imagined himself to have been a hero, and had a tendency to lapse into exaggerated tales of his heroic deeds on the field. But he was roped in, and eventually I followed the thousands of flag-waving fans pouring through the city to the MCG.

Despite the freezing night I was determined to give way to the pleasure of it. I could hardly wait to buy a four-and-twenty meat pie with tomato sauce and to cheer and holler at all the right moments. I did eat the meat pie, but it did not taste the way I remembered. Either they had changed or I had. The crust seemed hard and the meat was so submerged in gravy that it was gasping for its very life. Despite this, energy at the MCG was high. The jostling crowd was decked out with colorful beanies and scarves, brightening the night with flashes of color. Hand-knitted scarves flapping in the wind enveloped yelling fans.

I gave way as much as I could to the pleasure of it all, but most of the time the ball was far away on the other side of the oval, or at the other end where I could hardly see it. Either that, or the fellow in front was so loud that I could not hear anything above his raucous encouragement of his team. I was freezing and uncomfortable and very ready make my way home on the tram by the time the game was over. But I had done it. I had been to an Aussie Rules football game. And that was enough to satisfy me. Now I felt I was well and truly a Melbourne girl, but a Melbourne girl who did not have a need to do that again.

Mal was an Essendon football tragic. He and I were all of eight years old when we first met. He was all freckles and laughter and was still that way when he died. He was a skinny kid; I think all Australian children were in those days. We spent a lot of time at the beach, occupied with sand and sun, or at the local playground with its wooden-seated swings and their heavy iron chains, and we were happy with our own company. It was a good, carefree childhood. Our parents were friends. My dad had met Mal's father, Col, during their time of active service in the Air Force. Following World War II, Col became a wool buyer, and Mal chose to follow his father into that profession as a young man.

In the years before I returned to live in Melbourne, Mal developed a one-eyed obsessive attachment to the Essendon Football Club. Whenever we met again either in Melbourne or Los Angeles, Essendon moved to the forefront of the conversation. Mal was a salesman. It did not matter what it was he had chosen to have in his life, he would sell it to you. The benefits were extolled with determination and there was not a breath of an opportunity left for you to suggest that you might like or have, hope to have, use or hope to use any other: car, watch, toothpaste, computer, or roll of wallpaper. And so it was with his chosen and beloved Essendon Football Club. I sat through endless dinners where he extolled the virtues of players I had never heard of and coaches who had joined or left the club without my knowledge.

It was therefore no trouble to think of a gift for him. Anything with the Essendon colors of red and black would be welcome. A beach-towel? Red and black. A blanket? Red and black. Pencils? Red and black. A comb? Red and black. Any gift at all so long as it was the colors of the only team to barrack for. And I did find him a toothbrush once. I remembered this today over lunch when I commented to my husband that football clubs are very important to some people and seem to encourage a deep sense of belonging, which brings great pleasure. "You remember how Mal was?" I asked. "He even had an Essendon toothbrush. You know, a red and black one."

"I didn't know he had an Essendon toothbrush," Mr. T replied, looking slightly astonished. Mal had even parked his car in the same parking spot for every game for more than fifty years, and used to sell me on the reason why that was the only place to park if you were attending an Essendon game. Who was I to argue?

Mal is gone now. During the last few years of his life Essendon fell out of favor with him, a thing I could never have imagined. As the cancer which killed him addled his brain, he took to calling coach Sheady to tell him what he was doing wrong, and then to writing letters to tell him how to do it right. Eventually he settled on a punishment for their indifference to his ideas, and threatened to withdraw his membership, which he eventually did.

But the paper bag of life can also bring
moments of mortification.

ELEPHANT EGGS

Memories return of my student teacher days, with wooden floors in cold draughty classrooms with rows of desks sitting to attention. One class of forty youngsters—feet side-by-side on the floor, hands clasped on desks, and eyes turned towards me—sat subjected to my labored attempts to engage their young minds in the subject of nature study. At the back of the room stood the supervising teacher, casually observant. We had all just survived the lesson when an innocent child looking raised her hand, hovering it mid-air. It was my moment to finish with as much grace as I could muster.

Puzzlement showed on her face as she asked, "Please Miss. How many eggs does an elephant lay?" Drawn to disaster, forty pairs of eyes turned to her. Silence echoed loudly. Her puzzlement increased at the class reaction as, one-by-one, the pairs of eyes turned away, embarrassed for her. Her blue eyes filled with tears of distress. Something was wrong. The loud silence melted into childish giggles as the class waited for my response. Distress dribbled down her soft cheeks to her desk, and then as a flood of incomprehension came, all the way to the floor. I struggled for an answer that would save her. It was an inelegant moment, and her question splattered slowly to the floor with her tears. I was confronted with the harsh reality of the elephant egg size of her embarrassment.

A similarly embarrassing moment of my own had occurred in the rose garden of a woman to whom I had just been introduced. As we walked, she explained and pruned. She was a sweetheart, and blooming with the joy of new life. When I asked when her baby was due, she patted her belly. "Oh no!" she laughed, and I thought I might die right there amidst the roses. I promised myself that I would never ever ask that question again.

Some years of learning later I was enjoying coffee in Hellas Café in Richmond. Honey-scented fragrance mellowed all as sweetmeats in glass cabinets engaged me with their cornucopia of pleasure. I was mellowed too by the humming camaraderie of conversation and coffee in the emerging dawn. After musing over coffee, I went to offer my congratulations to the young woman who stood at the till, great with child. Her sharp intake of breath jumped across the space between us as I was dumped unceremoniously into embarrassment. Warning voices whispered. I had done it again. My eyes scanned her startled face, while somewhere on the wooden floor lay one of those elephant eggs, far too large to get back inside the box from whence it came, difficult to catch and uncomfortable to look at.

I was left feeling both gauche and foolish.

But laughter can be like medicine in the paper bag of life.

LINGERIE

With a little time to spare while in the city of Melbourne, I wandered into a favorite lingerie store to indulge in a fantasy of having enough spare cash to purchase one of each item displayed. Elegant and classy, all were to long for, to touch and to need. They were delicious. The young women who were there to serve gathered around as women can, to exclaim, comment, and laugh together at life.

The discussion turned to our corporate love of clothes, and the stories shared led to one beauty revealing that it was her godmother who first bought her a bra from this store. "They are amazing!" she grinned. We all smiled our pleasure. "I still wear it!" We smiled at her glee. "She bought it for my wedding," she added. We nodded in assent at the loveliness of the gesture. "That was fifteen years ago," she grinned. And we laughed out loud. "It has outlasted the marriage!" she tossed over her shoulder as she walked away to the back of the store.

LIONESS

Women share secrets, even inside the little paper bag of seaside stores.

It was a cold and blustery Saturday in the little seaside town of Dromana when I jumped into my car and whizzed off to my favorite thrift shop with a huge bag of no longer needed goods. Dromana sits between the foothills of Mount Martha and Arthurs Seat. At the end of Pier Street, the waters of Port Phillip Bay strove against the pillars of the pier, as lethally elegant stingrays, which had fascinated me in childhood swam lazily by. Tucked neatly near the end of Pier Street, the thrift shop was unpretentious. Signage that hovered mid-window alerted all who passed that this establishment was run by the Lionesses. It had been operating from these premises as a beacon of hope years before I ever found it and its covey of octogenarian helpers.

The folk who worked inside were charming in the way of those who had seen a lot of the ups and downs of life and survived with their sense of humor and generous spirits intact. They functioned in this small space with unaffected grace and inspired me each time I visited. Some unpacked, sorted and planned, laughed and gossiped, while others stood at the counter with watchful eyes, waiting for the sales which would support their charitable works in the community.

I have friends who share the compulsion to hunt for extraneous items in their cupboards and offer them to the thrift shops that spread out across Melbourne town. But one friend of mine loves nothing more than to take the burden of too many clothes off my shoulders before they ever have a chance to see the door of the thrift shop. She tells me that her daughter, daughters-in-law and granddaughters all love the joyful tussle of "who will take what" of mine. I am relieved of extraneous wardrobe and the women of her family are entertained with a fashion parade in my clothes. A few weeks ago, I told her that perhaps I would have to start giving my clothes to the refugees. She looked at me in horror and blurted out, "But we are the refugees!"

My Saturday morning trips to the Dromana thrift shop are more about dishes not needed, sheets not used, toys well past the use of our grandchildren, and books well read. I love the thrift shop most of all because of the hard-working men and women who volunteer there. Across the road, an enormous new thrift shop has opened its doors and has a far greater supply of offerings for sale. But in the Lioness's I find goods that are inclined to come from the estates of the local elderly who have breathed their last. Here the goods and their owners feel treasured, less discarded, and more handed-on. I come away with a smile on my face and the sweet generosity that pervades the place nestled into my spirit.

My need to clean out cupboards, drawers, and closets was satisfied for the week as I set off to deposit unneeded treasures. The last time I had visited, a lady rushed in from the street all of a dither and grabbed me by the arm. "I need some help," she gasped. "I can't carry all the things I have in the back of my car. Can you help me?" I must have taken on the Lioness's look.

Every time I visit, I determine that I will sidle out without making one single purchase. Yet I found myself asking the price of an enormous pink Easter rabbit with a colorful spotted bow adorning its neck. Offered for two dollars? I could not even begin to resist. Before I took my leave, I had to have one more look around to see if there was any left-behind gem which was just begging me to take it off the shelf and carry it home to love. I laughed at myself and my addiction to the hunter-gatherer lifestyle, and the Lionesses laughed with me. "Oh yes, we have seen it all before. You are definitely not the only one who does this!" I was momentarily relieved.

Standing behind the counter were two of the best. Eighty if a day, grey-haired, sweet-faced and sparky-eyed—they inspired me on my way down the aisle past the sheets, the books, the toys and on to the little room at the back where ageless angels sorted and gossiped, drank coffee and laughed. One sparky-eyed angel watched me on this numbingly cold day. She came hurrying towards me with a handful of necklaces I had only just brought in for their store. She wanted to be sure they were to be offered for sale. "Of course," I said, "but if you want any of them, take them home. The rest can go into the shop." The little cellophane packets of necklaces were quickly unwrapped and draped around one Lioness's neck after another.

A grey-haired charmer from the back of the store spied us and hurried over to enjoy the fun. She picked out one necklace and held it tenderly to her bosom. "Oh, I love it!" she smiled. Then ruefully gesturing, "The trouble is, you would have to have a big bosom to wear this."

"But look," I suggested, taking a length of the chain in my hand, "you could just toss it over your shoulder like this. It would look great on you."

She did not skip a beat. She grinned at me slyly and pointed, "You know," she said, "I could still throw one of my bosoms over my shoulder."

THE BOXER

He moves towards the pool with the awkward grace of one who is still struggling with the decimation to his body following a stroke. The left side of his body took the catastrophe, leaving his right side to cooperate more fully with his brain. His body is stifled along with his dreams by the suddenness of the changes. "I wasn't that good," he says of his boxing, "but it was all I ever wanted to do." He reveals parts of his heart to me over the top of the chlorinated water warmed to soothe our recovering bodies. "This is all I have left now," he tells me, pointing to the pool. "My son's in jail," he tells me another time. Then, "I gotta get off the booze," he admonishes himself as he explains the shiner I ask about.

He must be lonely, I think, to tell me such secrets. His stories pour out. They are urgent, anguished, abrupt, pain-filled, not wanting or needing a response. "Oh," is the only thing I can offer, and "Wow, Laurie!" as I let out my pained breath.

Urgency propels him, and he flees across the pool to my side to relieve the pressure boiling up inside. "You live in Richmond?" he yells—unbelieving, glaring at me fiercely. "Do you know the crooked cops there?"

"No, Laurie."

"I'm off the booze," he breathes into my ear. "Had to. I keep falling over. I think that's how I got this sore shoulder. I can't remember."

Pulsing away with his new story last week, he pushed his face very close to mine and started in. Then agitation got the better of him and he was in peril of not ever being able to release the words. "I had a ...," then, "I had a ...," then a third torrid attempt, " had a ... vasectomy. A vasectomy!" Then louder again. "I had a vasectomy. You know what that is?"

"Yes, Laurie."

"I had a girlfriend. The doc asked me if I wanted to have babies. "Gawd no!" I said, 'I'll be a grandfather soon. No thanks."

So he said, "Then you'd better have a vasectomy."

So I did. Now I've got diabetes! It gives it to you—it does. A vasectomy. It gives you diabetes. I asked my mum, "What have I got?" And she said I've got diabetes two. "It's diabetes two."

"Is that right?"

"Yeah," says Laurie emphatically. "That's why I got diabetes.

Then you know what happened after that? My girlfriend came up and put her arms around me and she whispered in my ear, 'Give me a baby, Laurie. I want a baby.' Why didn't she tell me that before? And now I've got diabetes."

CROSS BONES

Laurie battled across the pool. His boxing days were over, and even though he was heroic, I had never seen any improvement in all the years I watched him labor in the pool. I admired his determination, and wept as he confided, "This is all I have left." The stories he brought me weekly at our meetings in the pool spiked my soul with delight, a fizz of joy joining the artificial bubbles each time he leaned towards me with a "Have you heard?" story.

"Did ya see Brian Murphy last week, Jill?" Laurie leaned in conspiratorially as I waded across the wellness pool where the two of us braved an influx of strangers from week to week. Each stranger was grappling with some malady that did not sit lightly on his shoulders. Arthritis caused the knobble joints that would have looked more attractive covered over. For one, post-palsy delivered a blow so far below the belt that it hurt every part of the body and mind of the sufferer and his partner as well. Some weeks later Parkinson's was added to the horror diagnoses. Surgeries of every kind had brought pain ravaged faces in and out of our focus over the years that Laurie and I had entered these troubled waters. Laurie held his energy as high as he could as he battled the aftereffects of his stroke.

"They called him Skull. Yeahh!" He added, nodding sagely.

"Skull?" I raised my eyebrows to a height never before reached, although they been close to ceiling height before in the presence of brother Laurie.

"Yeah," said Laurie. "He was here last week. Didn't ya see him?" Laurie was amazed at my omission. "He has all kinds of cuts on his skull now too. He has! Had a few small strokes too, they say. Very famous he is. You've never heard of him?" Laure looked totally disbelieving. "He used to look after all of Brunswick," he said. "A policeman. Very famous. Very famous. Everybody knows Skull." He looked at me again, still disbelieving my ignorance. "He is famous for killing the British crim Raymond Bennet. They say he killed him. It was in all the papers. It was never proved. But he did it." Laurie nodded again at his own sure knowledge of this drama. He was contributing to my education and proud of it.

Laurie nodded again. Laurie knew a lot of things. "Yeah," he nodded in firm agreement with his own statement. "Yeah," he repeated. "Raymond Bennet hated him and told him that he was gonna kill him, see. Skull said, 'No you won't mate. I will kill you first.' Then there was this court case, see—and Raymond was brought in, see. They were just about to start when a bloke rushed in from outside all dressed up in a wig and a beard, and shot him dead right there in the court room. Yeah! Right there in the courtroom, in front of everybody. They never caught the bloke. But they say it were Skull that did it. Yeah." Laurie's eyes bulged with the joy of it all.

At home later I googled "skull." Apart from a few medical

descriptions such as that "it is a bony structure that forms the head of most vertebrates," I finally came upon a story. *The story*. Of a Melbourne policeman known as The Skull—Brian Murphy. Following a life of high drama, Skull has now written a book about his remarkable life. Or rather, Vikki Petraitis has written a book about Skull's remarkable life. *Once a Copper: The Life and Times of Brian 'The Skull' Murphy*. "Brian (The Skull) Murphy was one of the bravest and most influential policemen in Australia's history," says Vikki Petraitis in this biography. Now I am sorry I that missed The Skull at the pool. Laurie could have introduced us.

I will read the book, *The Skull: Informers, Hit Men, and Australia's Toughest Cop* by Adam Shand.

I have missed so much.

HEDLEY'S RIDE

Hedley was always a tall man. Good looking too, he had presence. He had style. Still does. Crinkly hair sprouted luxuriantly above his boyish face, both of which expressed his wickedly puckish good humor. Piercing blue eyes mirrored the puckish look.

The first time I remember smiling back at Hedley's great toothy grin was on a summer's night when a gathering of their friends were celebrating his latest girlfriend's twenty-first birthday. We were in country Victoria, and those of us who were city dwellers were relishing the country event. The night was balmy, and the skies were all dotted about with the myriad stars of the Milky Way. The exotic fragrance of country-gentry celebrations was in our nostrils along with the seemingly endless offerings of barbequed beef at its finest. Liquor was readily available, and the few Aussie blokes who had not yet learned to resist the call to show off by their excessive alcohol consumption, were into boyish revelry. The rest of us city slickers watched their hijinks and attempted to hone our "in the country for a weekend" skills. We felt as though we were preparing ourselves for a visit from Prince Charles to his country estate.

Hedley smiled at me from behind a beard of barbeque smoke and bonhomie. All six foot two of him was working both me and the crowd like a good Aussie cattle dog. He was charming and alert. He was garrulous at the same time as being intensely interested in all his guests. He was immediately likeable, a charmer on legs.

By the time I made Hedley's acquaintance that evening his life was already the stuff of legend. He had worked boldly to birth and nurture his remarkable successes. He continued then and continues now with his bold affirmation of life, and enjoys the products of his successes, not the least of which was eventually marrying that wonderful girlfriend. He has made millions. Lost a bit too. He has bought and sold hundreds of hectares of prime real estate. He has started up businesses and driven them forward. His friends marvel at his unstoppable enthusiasm, which leads me to say that along with his charm, his sparkling blue eyes, his generous hosting, and his good looks—Hedley is unstoppable.

The vicissitudes of life have occasionally perplexed and

plagued Hedley, but although he was sometimes baffled, he was never defeated by its challenges. He recovered. "Hedley always recovers," his friends said, "Hedley's strong." And so, it is.

Hedley still likes to tell remarkable tales, both tall and true. These days he tells his tales more than he listens to ours, but none of us mind for a moment. He is part of the old school of tall tales and shaggy dog stories born in the Australian bush. Most of his mesmerizing tales are true—some having become the stuff of legend along with the man—and continue to astonish even the meanest skeptic among us. He has a memory that settles into a tale with tenacity and verve and a complete disregard for anyone else's exotica. His own stories fascinate him, and if they have not been heard over and over again, they fascinate whomever he can bale up with that still intensely wicked, boyish grin. His stories never outgrow him. He continues to be larger by far than the sum of them.

I have to say Hedley is a gem. He is a one-off, a survivor. He is resilient, hard-working, risk-taking and dogged. He is always fun, and it could be said that you could sit with him over a meal and never have to open your mouth except to take a bite. He has never been known to run short of a story; he seems to know everybody, and those he does not know personally, he knows all about. He keeps those gathered fascinated. His memory for enticing statistics and scandalous detail fascinates him as much as it fascinates the members of his captive audience.

We all have tales to tell, but Hedley *expects* to be listened to. Expects the audience to pay obeisance. Expects a laugh. Expects to be the great entertainer, just as he was all those years ago at the country barbeque for his girlfriend. He is an endlessly interesting host. There is never, ever, a moment of silence around any table Hedley hosts. "Have I told you the story about _____?" he will begin, and we are off again on a roller-coaster ride scattered about with both disbelief and laughter.

Hedley fills us with his stories. By these he shows his love. "I will never allow you to be bored," he seems to say. "I do not want you to be sad today. I will cause you to smile. I will lift you up, and for this moment together we shall share laughter."

And so it was that as we six gathered at a North Melbourne watering hole for an annual catch up and gossip, Hedley was off again at a gallop. "Have I told you about being approached to participate in some filming?" he started.

"Yes," we all nodded, we had heard that story and it was a bit of fun, earned him some cash too. Good one, Hedley.

"No," he remonstrated, "I was approached again. Same people liked what I did last time. They were almost ready to start filming and told me that this time a bit of driving was involved. They also told me that I was to play the part of a cranky old man." His eyes flashed with joy at the memory. "I can do that," I said. "Will there be any dialogue," I asked?

"Oh yes," they laughed. "We want you to yell at the pedestrians. 'Get out of the way you bastards!'"

"Good," I said. "Can I say, 'Get out of the way, you f—ing bastards?'"

"No!" They raised their hands at me. "No! People can lip-read you know."

"Of course," said Hedley, looking crestfallen even as he related the story. "Anyway, they know I am passionate about cars, and a bit of fun in a fast car for a few more dollars? Sure. I'm up for that. Why not?"

"Have you heard the story of my being invited again to star in a film?" he asked again.

"Star? No! Really?" We were not very surprised. What would it be this time?

"Well, not exactly a film," Hedley demurred. His blue eyes twinkled and he moved in for the kill. The famous grin took up its Pepsodent bright position. He drew a deep breath in through his nostrils and let out a snort of a laugh. "It was not really for a film—it was for an advertisement. The company that approached me last time were pleased with the result of the first shoot, and I thought for a few thousand dollars I could do some more. When they explained that this time it would involve some risky driving, I was in. They had heard that I was a bit of a car enthusiast and wanted my skills.

"It was all a bit exciting. I had to be at the lot by 7:00 a.m., so I was up by 5:00 and on site by 6:30 a.m. I had hardly stepped out of my car when four cute young girls came running over to help me. Four girls. Four! They always seem to have four, not one or even two. But four! They were ready to do my make-up. 'Hey! Wait a minute,' I said. 'Can you show me what will I be driving?' I had thought perhaps it would be a Mustang or even a Porsche. They were raring to get me made up, and I was a bit ready to show off in the car."

"The sun was just beginning to rise. It was a bit damp and misty. 'You can see it, see, over there.' They pointed to the parking lot in unison. I peered through the morning gloom. I couldn't see a thing, the parking lot looked empty to me. I was more than a bit perplexed, so I looked all over the parking lot again and eventually had to ask again, 'Where did you say? I can't see a thing.' 'Over there,' said the four in chorus, pointing together like a group of cheerleaders. 'Over *there*,' they cried again, with an emphatic *there*, enough to convince me to try again anyway. I peered through the gloom again, determined to find my car."

As he moved to this part of his story, the famous Hedley grin seemed to slip from his face like snow melting off a warm windscreen. We at the table leaned in so as to hear better over the din of the pub lunch crowd. Hedley lowered his voice conspiratorially, then suddenly raised it to a crowd-pleasing crescendo. "'Hey!' I yelled. 'All I can see—is a wheelchair,' I said, 'an electric wheelchair.' *A bloody electric wheelchair!*"

A car or two has driven through my paper bag of life.

PICKUP

As a kid I had learned to drive with a combination of Willis's encouragement and a few lessons from a slightly older friend. I remember a few of the tricks I was taught. My favorite is the method for parallel parking, which goes down like good ice cream every time I use it, all cool and smooth and easy. "Wow!' said my passengers, "Where did you learn to do that?"

But my tried and tested parking techniques never did work quite so well in Rhode Island or Massachusetts or Chicago— or even in California. No matter how hard I tried I could never quite get the hang of a parallel park on what to me remained the wrong side of the road. My head and shoulders would protest loudly. My arms wanted automatic Australian mode, and threatened to bolt me and my trusty steed back into the oncoming traffic instead of taking us on a smooth glide, snug into curbside. I often gave up and took to the hunt for an easier space into which I could glide nose first, and out tail first.

The employment I had taken up in Los Angeles provided me with a living as well as a steep learning curve, but it did not include such practical things as furniture or a washing machine, which a single girl out there in the big wide world needs for a little comfort. After some weeks of fun searching in old barns, outlet shops, auction houses, and thrift shops, I purchased a few interesting items. Trouble was that they were some miles from home, in the town of Los Olivos, and delivery was not included in the price. I needed to borrow a pickup truck. There were so many things that a girl needed to do when she moved countries.

Larry was good guy and lived close by. I offered him the use of my big E-class Mercedes in exchange for his old pickup, and he was in like Flynn—with both feet. He stood, arms akimbo, with a huge grin spilling over his pudgy face as I backed out of his driveway. That grin could have been at the thought of a day in my car, posing. I did not mind what it was, I was off onto the Los Angeles freeways on an adventure of my own. Larry seemed to think it quite normal that the Jillian who wore smart suits and silk stockings should wish to borrow his battered old blue pickup truck with a stick shift.

I felt totally prepared for my journey, but to be absolutely sure I did not lose my nerve, I jammed Willis's old Akubra firmly onto my head and sallied forth. Friends from the bush who had, by virtue of need, their very own style of Australian school of driving, had imbued in me the need to know how to double-clutch and how to jump a dry creek bed in a pickup. What more could I possibly need?

The trip was interesting but uneventful until my cell phone rang. I was on the eight-lane Los Angeles freeway in a pickup, flying—with the stick shift hard at work—and wearing Willis's Akubra. Everything but everything was being managed in the true Aussie way. And the phone rang? I could not ignore it. I do not mean the hands-free, answer-with-the-press-of-a-button type of phone. In those days, hands-free was mandatory in Australia, but hardly heard of in California. The demands of my job required that I be at the other end of that phone at all times—day, night, and anywhere in between. Too much could be at stake if I ignored this insistent ring. There was I, negotiating the endless stream of Los Angeles traffic—traveling at 70–80 mph, changing gears, changing lanes, hanging onto Willis's Akubra, and answering the phone. I was definitely a sight to see. "Good material for a sitcom," I thought.

I loved it. Every person on the freeway seemed to be driving a pickup truck, and I was now part of a whole new community. Los Olivos finally emerged from the smog of Los Angeles. I parked the pickup and went off to find my furniture—only to discover that, despite my greatest effort at womanly determination, I could not lift the furniture onto the back of the truck by myself. Good fortune offered me a strong-looking gardener who happened to be walking past me and my dilemma. I accosted him and asked for help. When he took a good look at the furniture, he suggested that since we could not lift it by ourselves, he would be off to find someone else to aid us in our endeavors.

The three of us struggled and strained together. As we finished the tying on and all was settled for my return trip to Orange County, I asked the gentlemen where they worked on the property. "Oh, we do not work here," grinned one, as the other nodded. "We were just walking past."

A 993TT

I have also had Australian car adventures.

I enjoyed the company of a group of ladies at a monthly gathering that we called Book Club. It was a fairly loose term, but we did enjoy a good meal, a glass or two of fine wine, and some heated disagreements concerning the book assigned for the month. One night after aforesaid club, I kissed all goodbye and headed for my car. It was about 10:00 p.m. on a night that was both cold and windy—in the way it can be only in either

Melbourne town or the Antarctic. I was parked on Clarendon Street next to the Fitzroy Gardens, opposite Bishopscourt, and not far from the Epworth Freemason's Hospital. I walked rapidly to my car, ready for the warmth of home and bed.

Push little button on car key remote to unlock car. I did that. No response. Nothing. Push little button on car key again. Still nothing. Push again, harder. Frustrated now. Was there a flat battery in the remote itself? Many more pushes of that pesky button with no response at all from the car. The small red light on the key flashed in time with my now cranky pushing, grinning at me in the dark. Merciless. But the car was not playing this game. This car had a mind of its own. With no passing angels offering to come to my aid, I resorted to calling Mr. T, the penultimate car man. "I will tell you what to do," he said. Good! "Go to the door handle. There is a small plastic disc in the keyhole. Take that out and put the key in there. You will be able to open the door that way. It should be no trouble." The plastic disc was not hard to find, although I had never known about it before. I poked around and out it came, in went the key, and voila! I opened the door.

Trouble was, as I opened the door, I also opened a Pandora's box of flashing lights and yelling sirens such as could be used to wake the dead. As you can imagine, I was back on the phone again to my trusty husband, trying to hear his instructions over the cacophony of yelling, blaring, and bleating from my idiotically flashing car. "Talk to me!" he kept yelling. I was. "Can't you talk to me?" I was. This went on for some minutes until I understood him to be telling me to put the key into the ignition and turn it, and that all the bleating and blaring and flashing would stop instantly. It did not. Neither the bleating nor the blaring nor the flashing nor my beating heart. I was trying to keep my cool, see through the flashing enough to find a little black keyhole, hold the cell phone to my ear, talk to my husband, listen to his instructions, and hope all the time that I would not be arrested for trying to steal my own car. The noise inside the car was way past comfort level.

"Key in ignition?"

"Yes."

"Now, move the steering wheel back and forth a bit. That will stop it," said husband from far away in front of television and neither freezing cold nor going both deaf and blind. Thirty minutes of trying every strategy he had and it finally became time for me to call the RACV, which I did.

"You are not listed," they told me politely.

"Not listed? What do you mean?"

"Is your husband with you?"

"No."

"He is listed. But you are not. Which car are you driving?" I told him. "That car is not listed."

"Not listed? It must be." It was not. By now I was reduced to begging. "I cannot leave the car here bleating and blaring and flashing enough to wake the dead. I cannot start the car. Help me!" With that, all of a sudden, all the turmoil of the past half hour stopped, and a strange unsettled sort of peace descended on the car.

Into the eerie silence, "I tell you what," said Mr. RACV,

"your husband has been a member for twenty-eight years, I will send a truck."

"How long will that be?" I asked. I was a bit shivery with the cold and a bit shaky with the car's violent misbehavior.

"About seventy minutes," he replied.

"Seventy minutes?"

"Yes."

I hung up the phone and opened the door of the car to do a little pacing, when yes, off went the whole shebang again— lights flashing and sirens blaring. By now more than an hour had gone by, and not one person had come to see what was going on. On one hand I was grateful that I was not close to a residence because it was a truly pitiful noise, eroding part of my brain with every aggressive wave of sound. But on the other hand, I needed someone to offer a little solace.

Mr. RACV did eventually come. To my aid, I thought. But no aid for me that night. After thirty minutes of diligent trying, the best he could do was to turn off the sound. Temporarily. I still could not drive. The car would not start, and any attempt was met with such a blast of light and sound that it felt like the New Year's Eve firework display on top of Sydney Harbor Bridge. The next round of the rescue came in the form of a flatbed tilt truck. I could not leave the car in the street; I could not even lock it, but how would he get this enormous truck down our narrow little Richmond street, turned into our apartment's parking lot, and unloaded. The driver had come towards me all smiles and energy. At midnight? "And how are you this evening?" he grinned at me. I would definitely have to give him a better greeting to offer in such a circumstance.

With his skill and patience and good humor he did eventually drive close to home and part of the way down our narrow little Richmond street, but he could not even begin to approach the parking lot, let alone turn into it. The angels of mercy had been at work though, and there was one parking space available on that street, so that with a bit of muscle and good steering we three—Mr. T (who appeared out of the dark), the driver, and me—were able to maneuver my baby into that spot. By then the car was almost weeping with exhaustion, and so was I. The driver was glad to say goodbye and leave us.

Victoria's best electrical experts came the next morning to diagnose and fix my poor, soggy, little car. But no, it was beyond even them. A neighbor came out of her house while they were standing on the street beside my car trying their darndest to get it going and to stop the bleating and flashing. "Can't you stop that thing?" she yelled in disgust. "It's doing my head in!" Oh, I wish.

With the TT.

LITTLE BROWN BOMB

The colleagues I met while teaching at Saint Gabriel's School in Sydney were a wonderfully inspired, hard-working, eccentric lot. In mornings we labored with babies, toddlers, and tiny tots to help them find a path into the world of language and the use of their residual hearing. The children were bused in from various parts of Sydney and surrounds. In the afternoons, they were bused to their local schools to enjoy integrated classrooms with hearing children. After a quick lunch, the faculty raced for cars and drove off to visit the same children. We drove to a different location each day, and it entailed a lot of driving.

Willis had purchased a little dull-brown Datsun for me for four hundred dollars. The paint was so worn that it gave the appearance of a camouflage jacket on the dusty roads, and it looked so sad that there was always a whisper of anxiety in my ear as I drove the many miles. But never did I have one bit of trouble. That is, until I did. I had been to the Blue Mountains for my school visit and was driving home through attractive rural farmland when *chooffff*—up went a huge vent of stem from my car hood—huffing and puffing steamy trouble. The poor bedraggled little brown bomb came to a full stop. Frustration was my first reaction, but on glancing around I saw myself to be quite close to a farmhouse where I knew I would get neighborly help in the typically Australian way. As it was before cell phones had become our mainstay for communication, I trotted off to ask for the use of a telephone.

My knock on the front door was not answered, which surprised me as I had seen someone in the yard as I hurried over. More knocking, then waiting, then knocking again, until a shadow hovered behind the glass in the door that was opened, just a crack. The gentleman on the other side of the door was half turned away as though ready to run.

I explained my dilemma through the tiny opening and waited, while he remained very still except for his breathing. "I really need to use your telephone, please," I begged, as I explained about my poor droopy, hissing car. "I am stuck." He let out a deep sigh through his nose, opened the door slightly, and motioned me into the hallway. I stood, waiting to follow him to the telephone. But no, he was going to follow me, thank you! As I used his telephone book and made my call for help, he stayed close behind me, watching my every move. It was a bit spooky.

I thanked him and returned to my car to wait for car service to arrive. The tow truck brought with it a charming gentleman who diagnosed the problem, but needed to drive off to purchase a part. That was okay. I would wait in my car.

"Oh no, you will not," he said in no uncertain terms.

I was astonished. "I could just wait here and read," I suggested. But he would have none of it. That made me a little nervous. We purchased the part and returned to my little brown bomb, which he repaired, and I thanked him for his help, at the same time inquiring why it was that he insisted that I go with him.

"Anita Cobby was murdered right near here last week," he admonished. Ouch! It had been a hideous and gruesome murder, shouted about in all the newspapers.

No wonder the homeowner was reluctant to open his door. No wonder he insisted on walking behind me and not in front. No wonder he hovered as I looked for a telephone number and made my call. I felt big, cold, goose bumps. I wanted to hug the tow-truck driver. He had been determined to keep me safely with him. The murderers had not been found at that stage. He was not about to leave me on the side of the road by myself, reading.

I have been rescued a few times in my paper bag of life. I have also met a great variety of people in my paper bag of life.

FUNERAL HAT

"Oh yes! I know this kind of person," she nodded. I was sitting in Anya's home, the recipient of her lovingly prepared European style luncheon. Rye bread was from her favorite bakery. "Look how dark it is!" she said, smiling fondly, holding the loaf towards me. The salmon was from her favorite delicatessen. But the cucumbers? They were from the only store in town which stocked her favorite variety of the very best Polish pickles.

"Smells like Poland," I murmured as I was offered the jar for a ladylike sniff.

"Yes," she smiled, "smells like Poland."

All this is to say that I was sitting as a guest of the remarkable Anya, who had recently turned ninety-seven years old, returned from a trip or two to hospital, and along the way had informed her loving son in no uncertain terms that if he continued in his attempts to put her into a nursing home, she would call her lawyer. And she did. So up until now, she continues to reside and manage in her own home. I had been directed to sit on a chair in Anya's kitchen and behave myself by not offering to help. She insisted I only watch.

I sat, and we chatted as she moved from space to space—choosing, opening, peeling, chopping, shutting, fetching and carrying, and generally serving me.

At the table we continued our conversation about Anya's new book and new novel, my writing, her family, my family, her health and my health. Conversations with Anya are often provoking, always direct, and usually end up linked back to stories from her extraordinary life, about which she has written with great panache. Now the surviving children of her many friends who have passed on can become privy to the life their parents lived after they were gathered from various parts of the earth—including the ashes of the holocaust—to the shores of Australia to start their lives all over again. "It was hard," she said, looking at me meaningfully with her shining, intelligent, brown eyes—a little faded now from the years of her profound life. And that is all she tells me for now. She tells me what she wishes me to know. There is no artifice.

We talked on and I spoke of a friend whose behaviors were repeatedly and wearingly vexing for me. As I regaled her with my tales and pointed to one story as an example, she looked at me hard and said, "I know this kind of person." I could see that she did. By Anya's stern look it was obvious to me that I did not need to explain further. I was pleased that she was ready to listen, and willing for me to tell her one more story to illustrate.

My tale, tall but true, is the unbelievably bizarre story of the funeral hat. "This, is my funeral hat!" she stated emphatically as she adjusted a screaming pink creation onto her glossy locks. She had said it with such emphasis, she who had vexed me so often with her outrageous or inappropriate behavior. I turned to look. She had style; there was no doubt about that, as the Texans would say. Despite her stylish clothes and glamorous lifestyle, she had been a somewhat selfish person—but she also had a wicked sense of humor and could make me laugh with her at outrageous comments, disguising the barb beneath before I had time either to blink or think.

We were trying on hats, she and I, playing at glamour in preparation for the racing season. She slid her eyes sideways at me as she spoke, gecko-like, then up and away, with the obvious intention of not allowing herself to be caught checking out my reaction. There was no reaction from me; at least, there was no overt reaction from me. We could both play this game.

I was not about to give her the privilege of my overt response. I could already sense it was going to be beyond outrageous.

Not to be ignored or dismissed, she tried again. "This is my funeral hat!" she exclaimed, emphatic now with a hard edge of demand in both her voice and her body language. There was a dark hint of a smirk at the edges of her words. She looked directly at me, her head a little to one side to display the hat, beckoning my attention. Mocking. I could feel her covert clamoring for my shock—jealous for it, showing in the slight exaggeration of her breathing and the forced swish of her skirt. Emotionally she was strutting.

Funeral hat, I thought—what in the world is she up to this time? I moved myself away with studied nonchalance. As I did, she moved towards me with some distress-provoked agitation to catch me by the shoulder. She was preening now and utterly determined; head tilted back a little for better effect. She was grasping and gasping for my attention. She would have me obey, she who would be obeyed.

"You know!" she demanded, underlining each word heavily. "You know," she repeated meaningfully, totally unabashed, "this is my funeral hat."

I stepped back and turned towards her, frustrated now by her insistence. "What on earth are you talking about?" I asked, irritated and uncomfortable. And then as I started to turn away from her once more, I flipped the words over my shoulder again, deliberate and disinterested. I was doing my best to be dismissive.

"You know! My funeral hat!" She stamped her foot just a

little, emphatic and angry at my lack of attention to her inde-
cent pronouncement. She was not about to be rebuffed. She
came one deliberate step closer to me, chagrined by my lack
of respect for her not-very-well veiled reference to what I per-
ceived to be the fact that she was as-ready-as-anything for her
husband of nearly fifty years to summarily depart this life. She
would be prepared for the event, and this was exactly the right
hat for the occasion. She was ready. With her screaming pink
funeral hat.

It was just not nice.

"I don't know what you are talking about," I lied. But I was
in no way going to give her the benefit of my shock and horror, and I certainly was not going to move to laughter with
her at what she was attempting to disguise as another outrageous joke. It was definitely not nice. She huffed in frustration, turned and, taking the glamorous hat off, handed it to
the astonished shop assistant for purchase. And we moved on,
she and I. With life.

Three years after the unfunny funeral hat incident, her husband of by then more than fifty years, was indeed rushed to
the hospital, hovering on the brink of death. The diagnosis was
not good. He was so ill that the family was called. Grievously
ill, said the medicos. He may not last the night. We would consider it wise to call the family, they said. And she did.

The extended family gathered solemnly around the bedside
of this, their husband, father, father-in-law, grandfather, and
great-grandfather. He had been unwell for a good while, but as
the imminent possibility of death always comes too soon, they

mostly felt despondent and unprepared. But she of the funeral hat was well able to manage such a complex family situation. She was prepared. With the speed of light and hardly an intake of breath, she moved into martyrdom mode. "Don't leave me," she sobbed, tears streaming. On and on she sobbed and wailed, loudly, relentlessly. "Don't leave me!" The family shuffled gently in embarrassed agitation, like a penguin mob. Her little gecko sideways looks at them were very little, subtle, and deceitful through all those tears—and were not too obvious to most of the rest of the family. She was calculating, while they were grieving and shocked. It was all too much high drama for them to do anything except join in a quietly wailing chorus.

As the grieving chorus slowly began to gentle down, her adult son dabbed at his eyes with his white linen handkerchief, gathered his manly self back inside his crisp white shirt, and spoke just enough to calm the family—exhorting them to do what he knew his father would love, to sing a hymn together. There was the pale patriarch lying on his deathbed breathing his last. He who had been a well-respected musician was attended by the extended family and his already grieving widow, wailing and sobbing and begging her husband not to leave her. He had always loved to sing. In fact, the whole family had loved to sing together, harmonizing with gusto. They sang for him, cautiously and sweetly at first—after all, they were in a hospital—but they would offer this gift of mercy. They sang on then, with more courage and more vigor, buoyed up by their own melodies. Meanwhile, the weeper wept and begged again and again for he who was to have been honored with the funeral hat to stay and not to leave her.

This little grieving band stood singing, with the soon-to-be widow begging and wailing alternately, when what do you suppose?! He who was being mourned and caroled into eternity on the wings of song opened his eyes, smiled an angelic *just-returned-from-the-dead* kind of smile at the sight of his beloved family—and, moving his milk-white lips gently, started to sing along with them in his calm and clear baritone. It was *startling*.

Those assembled were startled into open-mouthed silence. It was incomprehensible. "It is a miracle," said the medicos.

"It is amazing! It is just like old times," said the family, beginning to sing again. Touching each other in astonishment and disbelief they wept and laughed into more song, as though it was just yesterday and they were all gathered around the piano at home, harmonizing with joy, overwhelmed, and very happy.

And she? Who knows or could imagine what she thought. She never did say.

And me? The last time I checked, that funeral hat was still in the cupboard. It has been a good seven years now.

I told Anya who smiled knowingly. "I have known people like this," she said.

HATS IN A TRUNK

When I left the shores of Australia for the first time, I carried with me the accoutrement of any self-respecting Feathery.

Hats. Many hats. Beautiful hats, all tissue papered for protection in a trunk that Willis had borrowed from an old Air Force friend, with a promise of eventual safe return. Hats matched the suits that traveled in another trunk. There was a turquoise silk number that sort of squashed down softly on one side. There was a fantastic red-white-and-blue number which complemented perfectly the white linen suit with its trim of wide red and blue tape down the front of the jacket and around the cuffs. That was my favorite. The brim was broad, white on top, blue underneath, and stitched in concentric circles. The band was red. I wish I had kept it. The turquoise one needed to go far away, it reminded me far too much of Merle and other ultra-conservative brethren ladies. I had more hats than any practical thing I took with me. I sure was indoctrinated with "the need to submit." The trunk full of hats was evidence of that.

Willis with Anne Miree and me, wearing a hat even then. The boleros Willis made while in rehab following his return from WW II. Penny the dawg was ever present.

Along with the hats, there has been coming and going of all kinds in the paper bag of my life.

O BROTHER, WHERE ART THOU?

He is such a sophisticated sort of bloke. My son Luke says, *urbane*. It's true. Well-traveled, too, in the way that only career diplomats can be. Funny, too, he is. And loud. And full of good stories. Terrific stories. True stories. And a memory! Not a moment of his fully lived life has been forgotten. Not a minute or a moment of the fully lived lives of his friends and his acquaintances has been forgotten either. Of politics he has a store of tales. Of history he has a multitude of carefully placed volumes in his head, all readily accessible.

But today the bloke needed a plastic bag. Of a certain size. In fact, he decided on reflection, he needed two. Did I have such? I produced an array. Most had been obtained from Ikea and hence ranked, Swedish style, according to length and depth, as well as color-coded to provide easy access for this girl in a kitchen full of things to do. He chose two. Dark grey they were. "These will do," he said, appearing well satisfied.

Some hours later, when he returned from the cemetery smiling and well satisfied with his afternoon's work, he regaled me with yet another of his tales.

"I have to deal with my brother," he had said. He almost never referred to "brother" by name. "I have to repair to the bathroom," he had said. And he did.

It appeared that at the cemetery they had wanted six

hundred dollars from the bloke to spread his brother's ashes. As far as he was concerned, this was unseemly. Another plan was hatched. Quickly. He would purchase a rose bush before visiting his family burial site. A little furtive planting and fertilizing, and brother should be permanently safe from harm. But on reflection, as brother had been a bloody bother for most of his life, at the last minute the bloke decided that the rose bush was more than brother deserved, given the misery he had put the family through for so many decades.

I began to understand that the bloke's need to repair to the bathroom earlier was to decant brother from his resting place in a decorative urn, into the two grey Ikea plastic bags. From thence brother was removed from our house that sunny afternoon to join the relatives in the family plot in the local cemetery, and thus to join his mother and father in eternal rest.

"By now, he is well and truly decanted," said the bloke when he returned from his second visit to the cemetery. He was smiling. He is a little wicked. Or at least he has a wicked sense of humor. Brother had been scattered or spattered or splattered, or whatever it is you do with a recalcitrant brother who has grieved you way beyond forgiveness.

So, there brother lies. In peace.

But the bloke had forgiven. Over and over and over again. For decades he had paid bills for unnecessary purchases after the bank had supplied a credit card one more time to a man without financial restraint. He had flown back and forth to deal with medical emergencies and their aftermath. He had purchased brother a home that was to be for brother's use for one year. The bloke was to go on for the next thirty years, paying all bills for the upkeep of that home. I looked on, constantly amazed at the bloke's good-humored humility.

Then just as I was wandering away in a reverie about friends and families and their stories, a startling thought took residence in my head. Brother had been "farewelled" with a fitting memorial service more than a month ago. I had attended. The bloke had flown in and stayed with us for some days to take care of all that. The lingering business and accoutrement following brother's life and death was over, and now the bloke was back staying with us again in order to settle brother finally but finally, into his resting place in the loving arms of his parents.

The bloke had stayed days and days in our spare bedroom. We loved his company. But where had brother been in the weeks in between that memorial service and today's decanting? I had never thought to look in the bedroom cupboard.

A SMALL FLAW IN THE PROCEEDINGS

The phone rang as I was reaching across the kitchen bench for a glass of wine to enjoy while preparing dinner. "Guess who this is?" I drew a blank but attempted to sound alert.

It was Sasha. We spoke rarely and I had not seen her since a luncheon almost a year ago. "What are you up to for Cup Day?" she asked.

"Nothing yet," I replied. "We are having the usual lunch," she went on. "It should be fun. Will you come?"

As we drove the long, dusty road to the luncheon I kept Mr. T occupied by telling him stories. "Did I tell you what Sasha said when she called?"

"No."

"I asked her how many would be coming to the luncheon. She named them. 'Just ten,' she said. 'What about the others?' I asked. 'Oh, they're all dead,' she said."

THE DECK

The Australian movie, *The Castle*, is the tale of an ordinary family who unite to fight injustice when an arrogant and bullying multinational group move to evict the family, demolish their home, and use the property for their own purposes. Justice prevails for the ordinary bloke as the family wins the fight. In the winning, their everyday home is transformed for them and for us, into *The Castle*. They are besotted with the joy of the win. We laugh and cry with them. My tale is of The Deck, another Australian icon, and a saga that began when The Deck, The Dragon Lady, and I came together one seemingly ordinary Sydney day.

I had purchased an apartment in a block of units balanced on the edge of a cliff and hanging precariously over Sydney Harbor, and The Dragon Lady was a member of the Owners Corporation committee for the complex. If I had had any idea of the impact of her redheaded self upon my life in the following twelve months, I would have done all in my power to avoid that meeting, and any other with her—ever.

I was on leave from my work in California, my mind occupied with many things. Time was precious. I had emailed her ahead, arranging to address the issue of annoying water penetration into my apartment from an unknown external source. Practical, competent Margie, who managed my other, tiny apartment, met me there early. When I watched The Dragon Lady arriving, I thought, "She is strong. She'll be able to present my issue to the Owners Corporation clearly." Our meeting was supposed to take thirty minutes. What followed almost took my sanity. She marched towards me, bosom aloft and red hair flaming. We greeted each other, conducted a cursory examination of the apartment, and I was preparing to offer my thanks and depart.

Then, with a sudden sharp intake of breath, The Dragon Lady thrust her bosom forward and declared, "*That* has got to come down! The Council has been. That is illegal. That is also unsafe," punctuating her wrath with jabbing fingers.

I turned to her in astonishment. There had been no lead in. I could not begin to comprehend what she was talking about. What was she pointing at? The door? The wall? Sydney Harbor? *What* had to come down? "That deck!" she spat at me. Margie and I turned to each other in astonishment. Neither she nor I had heard one single word about this until this moment. No letter. No memo. No phone call. Nothing. What was she was talking about? Margie, who had been standing a respectful distance away, now moved slightly closer to me and inclined her head for me to pay attention. Her proximity helped turn my mind from water penetration back to The Dragon Lady, whose fiery red hair was flaring around her head with righteous indignation. She was bristling with the importance of her pronouncement, and obviously waiting for my response.

"I am sorry." I said, "Would you please repeat what you just said?"

With one more heave of her ample bosom and an even more distinct pointing of the finger, "That deck!" she cried. There was a painful emphasis on *that*. Margie and I turned as one to look in the direction of her accusing finger.

"What are you talking about?" I asked, still polite, definitely puzzled, but not yet intimidated by her bombast.

"Your deck," she spat, enunciating each word with bitterness, eyes hard. I could not begin to take in the import of her statement. I fumbled for a reply.

"What do you mean?" was the best I could offer. "What on earth do you mean?"

"Your deck is illegal," she pushed at me, well into an obviously rehearsed harangue. "It has never been permitted, and it has got to come down. In fact, the Council is going to pull it down this week. I represent the Owners Corporation in this matter." At four-fifteen that Friday afternoon I stood transfixed by her awful sense of triumph.

But it galvanized Margie into action. "Quickly," she said, her face contorted with stress. "Now," she entreated, "you must go now! You must go to the Council offices now, and find out what she is talking about. This is serious."

I would come to live with the dread of each coming day and dealings with The Dragon Lady. She appeared in my life, and the result was that my legs turned to jelly and my mind careened, tortured, into a state of uncompromising stress. I felt intimidated by injustice and almost totally disempowered. Instead of the international hard-working girl, I was reduced to feeling like the four-year-old child I had been all those years before, running home from school in terror, chased by the boy next door.

For some years prior to meeting my red-haired adversary I had owned a tiny apartment perched on the northern shores of Sydney Harbor. It was the first home I had purchased entirely on my own. The views were splendid, but I had longed for a deck. From my window I gazed adoringly at the water and the moored boats below, waiting patiently for their owners to return. This apartment was a refuge and a comfort during a searingly bitter time in my life, my very own little piece of paradise. I had spent five years racing for planes to take me to the bedside of my aging and ailing parents while I lived in Sydney and they in Melbourne. I was "it", as well as working full-time and caring for the family when suddenly, after twenty-seven years of marriage, I was divorced. There was only one apartment available with a view of the water for the price I could offer. It became my own little castle. Built in the 1940's of red brick, it perched high on the edge of a cliff, riveted there over decades by the panorama and the welcoming lights of homes across the way. The walkway passing in front brought the sounds of adventurous folk who heralded the day with their energy as they walked from The Spit to Manly and back again. Inside I was safe. Outside I was free. It was all mine. The small wooden jetty to the right of the walkway was a meeting place for a group of grey-haired gentlemen who met daily to scrape paint or varnish from their old wooden boats and to gossip. The tiny beach to the right of that jetty was mostly mine, shared occasionally with a stately pelican. Shells, gleaming, golden, and as fine as butterfly wings could be found there rarely. I carry two dozen of these still, a handful of sunshine that has traveled the world with me, a reminder of the healing power of beauty and quiet. "These are the golden ones," I heard an elegant lady say of them. Together they were exploring the beach—she and her tiny blue-eyed granddaughter. "We are looking for the golden ones," she said. So was I.

Then unexpectedly, an invitation was offered to me to work in Southern California, with the challenge of a new life in a new land to draw me away from Australia and from the grief of a failed marriage. I went away from that magic place thinking that I would return very soon, but life took me on a much longer and more exciting adventure across the United States than I could ever have imagined. One year turned into two and ultimately into six—and I was still traveling the length and breadth of the United States for business. My CEO had said to me, "Tell me what your gifts are, and we will work with them." Up until then I had not thought much about my gifts, but the opportunity to observe and name them was liberating as I gathered up the reins for my role in public relations which brought me into the orbit of multitudes of high profile and successful people. I learned that I could manage any task that was offered. The steep learning curve was an adventure.

The time came for that tiny treasure of an apartment to be exchanged for a larger one, to await my ultimate return to Australia. I would have a bigger home to return to, and with a modicum of luck, a deck upon which I could survey the beauty of Sydney Harbor. And so it came about that a trusted friend stood representing me at an auction for another apartment that would eventually become mine. Throughout the auction we communicated by telephone, he standing on the deck of the apartment overlooking Sydney harbor, and I, trying to concentrate and be safe as I drove south on the freeways of Los Angeles in my trusty Mercy. I alternately cajoled and cursed into the telephone, and he won the apartment for me by bidding $20,000 more than the amount we had agreed upon. My $20,000, not his! "A rainbow surged across the sky as I made the last bid," he said in reply to my anguished pleasure at the result. "A good sign, I thought," he pontificated, smugly unrepentant, as I gasped my disbelief over the telephone across the unforgiving distance of the Pacific Ocean. "You will not be sorry."

Thus, a new castle with a deck firmly attached and an uninterrupted view through the Heads became mine. Owning it gave me a continuing sense of place. It felt like a hope-laden footprint in the land of my birth. It was my castle. My little piece of paradise. One day I would come back to live there.

View through The Heads from bigger Fairlight apartment.

The years rushed by, and still I was working in the sunshine heaven of southern California. Every year I returned to visit family and friends, and my little castle of an apartment—to check its condition and to imagine myself living there, watching the ferries plying their way back and forth from Manly to Sydney. I would return and sit on that deck

In the sixth year of my sojourn in California autumn returned, bringing its soft and gentle light. I was visiting family in Australia, when Melbourne town brought me the totally unexpected gift of a new love. We had known each other decades before, and the meeting again, the one-day courtship, the proposal and the marriage, make a tale to be told. A little bit of business to be done, a lot of visiting with family and friends to be enjoyed, and some drinking of champagne to be indulged in over a yarn or two. I felt that this autumn promised me all things good as I flew north from Melbourne to

Sydney, to meet she who came to be known as The Dragon Lady, and discuss water penetration in my apartment. Her apparent detachment when I explained the water penetration problem in my apartment, I took to be boredom. I needed her to represent me. But she had pointed to my deck, and nothing would ever be the same.

Down the hill to the council offices I drove in a state of bewilderment, my mind left somewhere at the top. I was still struggling to process the rapid change of agenda as I entered the Council offices. I was befuddled. "We are not allowed to tell you who contacted the Council about your deck," said the lissome young girl at the desk who had come to attend me. It did not take me much mental effort to guess just who it could possibly have been! "But someone here will be able to speak to you next week," she continued, sweetly unhelpful. By the time I explained that next week I planned to be back in Melbourne and hopefully in the arms of my beloved preparing for an April wedding, she began to sense my distress, and called Mr. Cool Council Person to my side.

No, I protested. I had not heard a word of this before today. No. I had received no letter, no phone call, no email, no nothing from the Council. Surely this could not be possible? What did I need to do now?' "Write," he said. "Write to us here at the Council. Write and explain your side of the story. Write soon. In fact, write very soon, or the deck will come down. The wheels are well and truly in motion. It appears that your deck never was permitted by the Council," he said, looking much sterner now and beginning to pronounce Council with a capital C. I felt decidedly glum. I also felt stunned, betrayed, perplexed, and astonished. Up until a few minutes previously, I did not know there was a story of any kind, let alone one with sides.

How long had the Dragon Lady been working on this devious business without me being informed? He was not about to tell me. The deck had remained serenely where it had been for decades, surveying the starry nights and the bustling days as ferries plied their old ways back and forth to the city. St. Patrick's proudly dominated the cliffs opposite. The Heads guarded us all as they had done for centuries.

Who knew my deck's history? Who were those eager conspirators who had first dreamed of her, and worked to bring her to life? Who had sat on her over the decades? What stories could she tell? What secrets did she hide? And what did The Dragon Lady want with her destruction? For days, then weeks, then months, the Council wound its weary way through the items relating to decks listed in its box of complicated rules, regulations, and restrictions which had all come into play with Bren guns blazing. They became those who told me what to do with my deck—when, where and how I should do it—why I should do it—and how I had nothing to say, or think, or expect, or hope for that might make sense in the worlds which existed outside their hallowed halls. I indulged in letter writing that was creative and curt, frustrated and frustrating, calm and academic, short and to the point, long and to the point, dizzying with repetition, and stating and restating the facts.

I badly wanted the deck to remain where it was to weather many more Sydney storms.

And then one brighter day, the managing agent discovered that The Dragon Lady had acted alone, totally without Body Corporate approval. She had used their letterhead in a devious effort to hoodwink the Council. She did not represent them at all. She had moved so quickly that she had taken it upon herself to call in workmen to demolish the deck. She had even gone so far as to give orders to the workmen to place bolts on my external doors. I discovered, too, that she had lobbied other residents with fabricated tales about me. I was living in the middle of a nightmare. The Council had moved well and truly to her side. They became entrenched in their view that she was right, that the deck was illegal, and had to come down.

Until, by virtue of more determined investigation, her devious self was slowly being revealed. What did she want? Even Mr. Cool I Know Everything and I Am Always Right council person was beginning to look a little bewildered.

I discovered that mine was the only apartment in the block with a deck. Even the Dragon Lady did not have one. She was jealous! With this new information and a gathering of anger and frustration, I moved to challenging the Council about the permitting. Yes, they had done a thorough search, they protested, and there was definitely no permit for the deck. They were absolutely within their rights to plan the demolition. Papers with orders for demolition had already been mailed to me. It did not matter a bit that I had not received them. That was not their problem.

I had been accused of covering up something illegal. I had been made to feel like a fraud and a shyster, and I did not like that feeling. My frustration increased with the escalating aggressive attitude of Mr. Council. His posture indicated clearly that he believed he was on high moral ground, despite the fact that he was willing to admit that he had believed The Dragon Lady without checking her claim to be representing the Owners Corporation. "But she was extremely well spoken, and very persuasive," was all I was offered as an excuse.

Margie's hard work and mine finally brought me to the point where I needed to call an Extraordinary General Meeting of the Owners Corporation. After notice of the meeting had been sent to all owners, I received a telephone call from a gentleman in Tasmania. He was an owner too. I had never met him. "What do you need from me?" he asked. "They are a bunch of old biddies up there. I inherited a couple of units there from my Dad. I needed to do some work, new kitchens and such. In order to do the work, one brick in an external wall had to be removed. You would not believe the fuss. You have my vote." His calm sanity and wry humor were a welcome gift.

One more flight from Melbourne to Sydney for the Extraordinary General Meeting ate into my brief wedding preparation time. The chosen venue for the meeting was in the dismally cold covered-carport area, where the Body Corporate members came through the darkness carrying folding chairs and hostility. I had not yet lived in my apartment and therefore did not know even one of them. Down the hill they came, across the lawn, and into the fray. Of the whole lot, only two nodded a moderately polite "Good evening." I shivered with anxiety and cold. They banded together for comfort, as though I offered some kind of real threat to their lives. What had been said about me? What had been said about the deck? Two of the older women, fragile and grey, looked like chooks on a swing, bending and craning to look at me while attempting to appear balanced and calm. I, too, was attempting to appear balanced and calm.

Anxious to return to all that was unthreatening and familiar, the assembled group could well have provided the cast for a sitcom. The best-looking gentleman of the lot, dressed impeccably in a navy pinstriped suit and with suitably gelled hair, appeared lawyer-like with a portfolio of papers as big as my own. The group hovered close to him as if for protection. Closer to me, but definitely not close, was a ruddy faced gentleman with his comforting looking spouse. I tried for my best "I am not afraid of you" look, and endeavored to calm my breathing as the rain trickled down at the edges of the carport forum. My heart palpitated anxiously within.

The meeting of the gathered throng was chaired into submission by he of the pinstriped suit, whose manner was accusing in the extreme. His tone was impersonal and he was not at all impartial in his outlandish statements. "You have a deck which has never been permitted," he started out, "and it is therefore illegal. However," he continued, smiling in a smarmy way, as though he was bestowing me with gifts, "we have met to discuss, and then to vote. We will decide whether the deck can stay in principle, simply because it has been there for eighteen years, or whether we will tell the Council to proceed with the demolition as planned."

The level of palpable hostility in the room increased. Discussion became pointed. I was all but called a liar. I was berated for keeping the illegality a secret. The Dragon Lady had duped many there, and I had little in the way of facts to present. I had no copy of Council permitting. They had told me that they had searched, and that the deck did not exist. I needed cold, hard facts. I needed evidence of an original approval. The managing agent had spent two days searching her records to no avail. A horrifying five-thousand-dollars-worth of legal council had been purchased by me to aid and abet my fight.

Most of those gathered under shelter in the carport looked as though they wished they were not there. They also looked as though they wished the deck was not there either. Few could look at me. Few smiled. No one welcomed me. No one shook my hand. No one offered me a seat. The deck that they had not noticed for nearly two decades suddenly loomed larger than life and appeared to be threatening their serenity. Now they would have to think about it. Now they would have to make a decision about it. The Dragon Lady had pointed to the deck they had never noticed and then, like a magician, offered them the chance to be rid of it. The dripping rain exacerbated my misery. I was made to feel like an alien by their coldness toward me. Many of the residents had lived long in this apartment complex where views were proud and compelling. Vast expanses of water sparkled in summer as ferries as strong as oxen braved their way through the waves. They owned those views, and up until now with my ownership not visible to them, I did not. They had the right to their say by dint of long-term ownership. Their grey-haired history showed clearly in the gloom of the night.

Relationships of neighbors offered comfort, but not to me. I was excluded from this gathering by the lack of greeting, the lack of eye contact, the lack of welcome by the chair, and by the dense formality of the proceedings. Mr. Pinstriped Suit, who I discovered later to be in the employ of The Dragon Lady, smiled at the group, then glanced at me briefly, looking smug. There were a few tentative smiles back to him. Most looked anxiously about or cast their eyes down as I took my courage in hand and looked at each in turn. The Dragon Lady was very far away from the carport, sailing the seven seas, he informed us. "I am speaking for her," he offered. He was so self-assured. So confidant. So sure he was so right, and so pleased with himself.

There was brief and pointedly uncharitable discussion about the deck and me, then a restless scraping of chairs as we moved on from the discussion to time for the all-important vote, when from behind me on the right came the melodic sound of a deeply male Irish voice. He with the comforting-looking wife and the ruddy face lilted into the conversation with all the courtesy of the Irish gentleman. "Before we vote," he said, "I believe, in Australia, it is the usual way to give folks a go. Why don't we give her a go." He was talking about me. I wanted to hug him.

Like a ray of sunshine his words began to penetrate the consciousness of those gathered. And mine. One of the frail older ladies I had seen when they first walked in seemed to gather strength from those kindly words. Dressed in a soft grey flannel skirt and a pale blue twin set, she held her hand gently forward in a pleading but courageous sort of way. Apparently comforted into confidence by the way the conversation had moved, she spoke up timidly. The residents deferred to her age and silence reigned as, "I think I remember the deck being approved about eighteen years ago," she said. Quietly.

That was all. There was such a thunderous silence that I thought the roof might cave in. The sound of dripping rain faded. *What did you say*—I wanted to shout. I watched in amazement as the huddled throng agitated like spooked cattle at this emerging information. Their faces began to show horror at the thought that they themselves may possibly have been duped. By dint of the sheer force of her personality, The Dragon Lady had galvanized them into a frenzy of oblivion to any possible facts. Facts, which they had not for a moment stopped to consider.

These few words, spoken so softly, were a proffering of hope for me who up until now had stood completely alone. *Now*— I heard the slight scraping of chairs seem to comment at her words. *Now, they might be shown up for what they have been, weak people looking for power in a very small place.* The chairs scraped again as they who had so reviled me and the deck, endeavored to turn away from the conflict. *It wasn't me who wanted your deck down,* their chairs suggested. Grey heads bobbed. Half smiles replaced the looks of power and triumph that had dominated earlier. A palpable sense of personal horror seeped in at the thought that they might just have judged the situation too quickly. Heads turned this way and that. Eyebrows, which had been intensely furrowed, now raised in surprise, then lowered furtively to hide the same surprise.

Mr. Navy Blue Pinstriped Suit had been caught with his pinstriped pants well and truly down by this contribution to the proceedings. He had come unprepared for a fight. Now here was The Dragon Lady's toy-boy spokesperson, and suddenly things were not going according to plan. He had been all ready for a win. He had been so sure of himself that he had not expected any support at all for me. He could not work out which way he should proceed. He drew in a deep breath and tried in vain to cover his possible exposure. I wanted to smile at his obvious discomfort. As he endeavored to recover his composure, vote they did—this motley crew who had come so determined to see me put in my place, to determine whether the deck could stay in principle, with legal details to be sorted out at a later date. Yes, vote they did.

And I won.

To everyone's amazement including mine, I won. We had a stay. In principle, the deck could stay right where it had stood for eighteen years until I had the time to investigate further, and one more chance to uncover documents to prove the validity of the deck's approval. I was quietly and reverently ecstatic, but unwilling to shake hands with those gathered into a change of heart, for fear I should show too much enthusiasm.

The words of the thoughtful Irish gentleman and Mrs. Shy and Courageous had saved me, and could possibly save the deck. Mr. Irish's encouragement to "give her a go" had moved what felt like mountains of resistance. Whatever forces had gathered in the depths of her memory to summon such courage, Mrs. Shy and Courageous had continued the turning of the tide. I felt I was on a roll, well and truly over the first hurdle and on my way, bit clamped tightly between my teeth. The deck may just stay to weather another Sydney storm.

I still had the Council to deal with. I was beginning to feel as though I may be heard by the Council. I started to feel release. But I needed a handful of cold hard facts. I needed evidence of that original approval.

"Just how far back did you check?" asked Mr. T, gritty with exasperation. He had flown to my aid, bringing with him much more complicated dealings with councils than I had ever experienced. We were back in one more meeting with the Council, in an effort to prove one way or another the verity of the permitting.

"All relevant papers in this office have been checked," declared Mr. Council, hoping to get me out of his hair for good. He turned his head slightly to his colleague, smiling as graciously as he could in an attempt at a wordless apology for all the effort I had put in.

The words, "in this office," stood at attention in Mr. T's mind. "In this office?" My mind took one step forward, in for the kill. "In this office?" I demanded. I stared at him, as we dared him to reply with truth.

"Is it possible there could be any more relevant papers in another place?" Mr. T asked, gritty with angst.

"Well, we do have archives, but they are not housed here," he replied, glancing at his colleague in a wordless plea for help. They nodded to each other as if in agreement. "Whatever do you expect from us?" they seemed to say.

"Oh, really? Were they searched?" I demanded with a strong emphasis on the *they*. Embarrassed silence filled every corner of the small office. I did not care. His breathing changed. So did his colleague's. So did mine. But while they breathed deep and hard, I waited, a little cold and more than a little hostile.

"That would have taken a lot of time and we are understaffed here, as you can see," he offered, apologizing with a wave of his hand, "and we are extremely busy. There is unlikely to be anything relevant there anyway."

"Unlikely? Unlikely? After what you have put us through, you tell me you have not done a complete search because you are busy? I am busy too! You will search today!" I heard Mr. T demand, cold now. Hard. Mad. Furious, in fact. Could he possibly mean what he said?

The Council was planning to demolish my deck without me even knowing about it, and he was talking about being understaffed and busy? "You have put me through hell for months, and now you tell me you did not do a complete search for the permitting? And yet you made a judgment and took action against me on the say-so of a lying woman, with the excuse that she was well-spoken and well-dressed?" I was stupefied by the insanity of the whole situation, and this revelation was the final straw. I was way past being polite or patient.

"I have another meeting to attend now. I will return in two hours. Have the search completed, or I will sue," Mr. T blasted at the two of them as we stood up abruptly and left.

And so it was, that the morning after the Extraordinary General Meeting of the Owners Corporation, with my plane for Melbourne due to leave by early afternoon, and one more appointment with the Council officers due after their final search of the archives, I drove across Sydney one more time to the offices of the Strata Managers in order to search through a dusty twenty years of inordinately boring minutes of meetings, in the hope of finding any smidgen or scrap of real live evidence of the original approval of the deck. There I was shuffled into a private room where a rather apologetic Strata Manager presented me with two enormous piles of minute books and a promise to return with more. She had been sympathetic, and she had tried to be helpful. They had already been searched at my request, over a period of two days, and there was no evidence of a yes vote for the deck. Absolutely no evidence. Too bad. Yes, too bad. For me.

Left alone while she went to collect the books of minutes, I prepared to wade through what felt like quicksand towards a table laden with minute books. I was worn down to the nub emotionally and physically. I jammed reading spectacles onto my nose, slapped myself into a seat, and reached for the top minute book. As I touched it, it opened itself lazily to a central page with dates at the top as old as my apartment. And there I read, so simply, so completely, so impossibly, the very meeting notes I needed. The deck had been approved. It was all there in black and white. I had not been in the room two minutes. It was surreal. It was all so very quiet and so very ordinary.

By the time the apologetic strata manager returned to the room with another armful of minute books, I was laughing and ready to hug her. I felt somewhat hysterical. There had to be an angel of minute books somewhere in that room. The strata manager looked at me, startled and uncomprehending as I thrust the minute book towards her, laughing and pointing to the date of the approval and not resisting the temptation to cry.

The Council meanwhile, did search their archives, and they did find the permit and approval for my deck. The Council did rescind the order to demolish my deck. And the Council agreed that they had been way out of line. And eventually the Council did write me a two-page groveling letter of apology.

It had been weeks of anguished work. But I did have my apartment and I did still have the deck. By now even I was amazed at the outcome.

But I had one more pressing need. I needed The Dragon Lady to go very far away from me and from my deck. I needed her to wash her mouth out with something very strong. I could not expect an apology, despite the fact that I thought for a while she would take not only my deck but also my sanity. I needed to drink a bottle or two of good champagne with friends and my beloved, and then buy the world's best shampoo, jump into the shower, and wash that lady right out of my hair.

The Deck would preside over many more Sydney sunsets, observe many more Manly ferries filled with day-trippers, many more storms and bursts of sunshine, many more barbeque gatherings and elegant dinners, much more reveling and laughter, and many more quiet moments of peace and reflection.

Ultimately, I had had a fair hearing. But I still had a lot to learn about the art of fighting for a fair go.

I have sometimes been a bit of an idiot as I have tried to breathe deeply of the air in my paper bag of life.

FIRST CLASS ELEPHANT

I stood with a small cardboard box in my hands, looking at my own private financial crisis. Wrapped in brown paper it looked deceptively innocent. Not much of a girl for purchasing on the Internet, I had allowed myself to be seduced by the images from the *New Yorker* magazine and Condé Nast. Capricious copies of older magazine covers, flamboyant and fashionable, had teased me into activity. I had smiled as I explored page after enticing page.

Seven years of my life I had lived back east in the beautiful New England states of the US. New York had thrilled me then. It thrilled me now. My three sons had been born there.

One was buried there. A quiver-full of memories nourished my imagination.

But on this bright morning, having been transported back by life's command to Australia, the country of my birth, I found myself standing, brown cardboard box in hand, stricken. Choosing with care, I had perused the items of great elegance for sale on the Condé Nast site. Not a sparkle of stress flickered through my mind as I tossed a few into the cart. All the items I had chosen belonged inside my heart as part of memories of a life gone by. But I was shocked into disbelief when the total cost popped up on my screen. I was forced to backtrack, curb my good taste, and eliminate more than half of the chosen gems. With only the very best left in my basket, and concentrating deeply, I moved step by step through the minefield of unpurchasing on the Internet.

More disbelief as I looked with increasing desperation for a way out. How could it be that the cost of postage from the US to Australia was more than twice the cost of the short list of items chosen? Heaven help me. There must be a way to back up and out of this. One more step, but the way out was not there. Breathless with misery I went through to the bitter end of the whole process and was locked in forever. I had paid for postage enough to send a small elephant around the world first class. I felt imprisoned. The Internet police would come to get me, knocking at my door any minute. I could feel it.

Gathering the last of my courage around me like a warm dressing gown, and in repentant desperation, I put mental pen to paper and sent a begging email to customer service at Condé Nast. "This is my story," I said, Please help me."

And they did. The heavens opened with their mercy. The sun shone again. I could breathe once more. "We can cancel the whole order," they offered, "and you can start over." I wept silent tears of relief, wiped them, started over, canceled the order, and went to bed sadder but wiser.

The insistent doorbell two days later caroled warning. I should have known it was all too good to be true. I was left riveted to the floor, my trembling hands grasping a small brown cardboard box from Condé Nast. It was not possible. I had canceled. They had canceled. Shuddering thoughts attempted to gather themselves into sentences in my mind. Cold feelings invaded my chest. Something had gone terribly wrong. I stopped breathing.

The innocent looking box once deposited on the kitchen bench was a cardboard time bomb. It had garnered a life of its own, unsought and unwanted. It was like an orphaned child trying its best not to be noticed. But it was in the way, most particularly of my sanity.

Gathering all the courage I could search out so early in the morning, I compelled my legs to move towards the computer one more time. How could this have happened? How could this be resolved? I dared not breathe. Message sent, I complicated my day with useless activity. As day turned into night, and night into day, the true, bright, and clean colors of Condé Nast beamed out across the world from the East Coast of the United States to the East Coast of Australia. "Your debt is forgiven," they emailed. "Enjoy your goodies," was the substance of their message, "We like to look after our customers."

Talk about integrity, I said to myself, and to them via email. "Genuine selflessness too," I said. The story says volumes about the company and about the representative who helped me in my misery. It says more than all the clever marketing gimmicks in the world. The old fashioned *we forgive* was full of life-giving power. I was released. I could breathe again. I felt refreshed, renewed, and reborn. I would do this for someone else. I would forgive without resentment. This was true redemption. I still have not opened the small cardboard box. But I have opened my heart.

There have been challenges both small and large
in my paper bag of life.

UP A LADDER

I really do feel as though I am what my beloved friend Doug calls "up a paddle without a creek." Doug has dementia now, and although I have not seen him in this state, it grieves me. His wife Jane tells me that his ridiculous sense of humor still prevails to the point that some folk do not perceive the dementia.

Jane is a nurse. She does. Perceive the dementia I mean. It was first obvious with his driving when he would forget how to find his way. But now I am up a paddle without a creek myself, and it is all self-inflicted. A good friend Marcia took it upon herself to send me a jigsaw puzzle. I love puzzles. I do not know if Marcia even knew that, but there it was, all wrapped up like a Christmas pudding in cloth. The quality was terrific. The pieces did not tear as they were separated even though they were tiny, each being about one centimeter square. There were one thousand pieces.

I jumped right in, and in three days, with Mr. T's help the puzzle was complete and I was beaming. I loved every twist and turn of the procedure. So inspired was I, that to the computer I ran and ordered myself the puzzle with the largest number of pieces I could find. Six thousand pieces it was, portraying the Sistine Chapel ceiling. It sounded like puzzle heaven. In the weeks since I purchased it, I have learned a thing or two, but I am beginning to suspect that I have a thing or two more to learn. As I sift and sort the tiny pieces, I think daily about Michelangelo up that ladder doing his thing and I want to find out more about what drove him. As I sit at the table with my puzzle, certain mantras roll over and over. Like this: *Red—look for red—only red.* Then: *Green—only green—look for green.* No one can hear me because I do not say it out loud. But I can hear me, and I laugh at myself and know that if anyone could see into my mind they would laugh too.

The best discovery I have made in all these days of joy is that I did not think to check the dimensions of the finished puzzle before I ordered it. You can imagine my howl when I discovered that as a completed puzzle it will not fit onto our dining room table. Since that is the only table we have, apart from a glass coffee table and a far smaller round wooden table, the puzzle is still on the dining room table while I pray to the puzzle gods that the whole thing will shrink as I put it together.

Tonight, I had a bit of a go after dinner. Mantra, mantra, mantra. And all I managed to do was join two pieces. By my calculations, at the present rate the best I could possibly do would be to complete the whole thing in ten years. Six joined pieces a day by, let us say, four days in any given week equals twenty-four. Twenty-four times forty, which would be the possible number of weeks I would be here to enjoy it, makes approximately one thousand pieces a year. So maybe I am exaggerating. Maybe I could finish in six years. This, of course, is barring floods, fire, and pestilence of various kinds.

I need to take a break and find more about the master himself, Michelangelo.

We went to Rome once, and while there did wait in a queue with thousands and wandered through the Sistine Chapel with the same thousands. There was not time for reflection, which is a pity, and I am left only with the enduring memory of a priest outside the Vatican toting a rather large plastic shopping bag on which was emblazoned a photo of the Pope. It tickled my fancy, so, I took his photo, and he scuttled off like the proverbial startled rabbit. He looked *caught*. I would love to have known what was inside that plastic bag.

But now at home I am stuck, mentally craning my neck upwards to see what Michelangelo was up to, that he could so prevail to produce all the ravishing love which has endured through so many decades to still bite at our heels with bliss and harmony. Wikipedia tells me that "the complex design includes several sets of individual figures that have provided an enormously influential pattern book of models for other artists ever since." What a lot of twaddle. "Pattern book," indeed. I cannot believe that such tripe could possibly be the motivation or expected outcome of Michelangelo's crucifying stint up a ladder.

In the early sixteenth century he was an esteemed artist known throughout Italy. Pope Julius II hired Michelangelo in 1508. I read that he took the commission reluctantly, and that two artists, rivals of his, hoped he would fail, since he was less accustomed to painting than he was to sculpting. Nasty. He took a yearlong break in 1510 and completed the Sistine Chapel ceiling in 1512.

In order to manage the challenge, Michelangelo created special scaffolding, which was designed to move across the chapel in stages. To me, it sounded like a lot of hard work altogether, apart from the painting, but I am relieved to discover that the platforms on the scaffolding allowed him to paint in a standing position.

So there I was typing away in a frenzy of anxiety about poor old Michelangelo, not beloved by fellow artists, consumed with a commission to paint when what he really wanted to do was sculpt—in one way or another up a ladder without a paddle, or whatever Doug might say about him. I was ready to rush off to Rome with a cup of tea and a vegemite sandwich, or a hip flask of whiskey if he was so inclined. Anything, I thought, to help him complete such a "forbidding task." But Wikipedia reassured me that the poor man was not so poor, as he did not in fact have to lie sweating on his back atop his rickety scaffolding. How they knew that he was in fact able to stand up, they failed to explain. Off I went on a Google hunt looking for more answers. Standing for four years painting away did not seem to be quite as bad as lying on his back painting for four years. Pretty bad though. I would forget the vegemite sandwich and just proffer a cup of tea.

But as I was saying, there I was typing away, somewhat agitated about my purchase of a six-thousand-piece puzzle, the too-small dining room table, Dick's dementia, and Michelangelo's dilemma, when KABOOM! Up on my screen rose terror. In huge red letters, followed by equally huge exclamation marks I was confronted with:

Trojans!

Beware!!

Close your computer immediately!!!

Three Trojans have invaded your computer!!!

Close immediately!!!

It felt like the beginning of atomic warfare.

All I had been doing was searching various Vatican websites seeking information enough to give me the courage to go back to the dining room table and my puzzle. Someone was surely out to get me. Maybe it was Michelangelo's enemies, the jealous artists.

A good night's sleep later, a trepidatious opening of my computer, and voila!! No red terror. It is all enough to give a girl the courage to rush back to the too-small dining room table and the too-large puzzle—and find a creek, any creek, to help me with my paddle.

"To think," said Mr. T, "that it took Michelangelo four years to paint that ceiling, and it might take you six years to complete the puzzle."

RICHMOND GRIT

"What a lot of hopeless idiots my friends are. Every last one of them." There I was sitting at our beautiful dining room table fuming not so quietly to myself.

The beautiful dining room table was designed by Mr. T. It is constructed of special glass, bumpy in an interesting way underneath and smooth on top. When it was being manufactured by one of Mr. T's clever friends, the glass broke twice. Once ready to deliver and brought to our home, it was discovered that the whole thing was too large to fit into the elevator. Back to the drawing board and a new design was produced, now in two joinable parts. Up in the elevator it came, as did the interesting metal support structure with its own wonderful set of wheels for moving the table hither and yon.

These days it is little used for dinner parties, however it does have a grand capacity to collect dust. But not just any dust. This is Richmond dust. Really it is Richmond grit, which creeps in through tightly shut windows and doors to lie in wait for me, slightly oily from all the trams which rattle up and down Bridge Road and Church Street, and slightly black from the traffic which rattles down the same streets along with an ambulance or two screeching its way to the Epworth hospital, transporting some poor soul trying not to breathe his last. Oh, and the fire engines. Richmond seems to have an inordinate amount of fires, unless they are just practicing.

So there, I was fuming. I was mad. Really mad. Not one single friend had come to my aid to help me with my six-thousand-piece puzzle. "The trouble is," I mooned, "a lot of my friends live in other countries or states, and are not inclined to visit."

So I miffed away. (Can you *miff*, away? I like that.) But so dogged and determined I was as I ruminated and puzzled over the puzzle, that I would not allow my husband to repeat that I word in my presence.

Puzzling away on our dining room table.

"*Impossible*," he says, a little mocking and a little perplexed by my persistence.

"No, it's not," I retort, head down, focused. "Challenging," I say, daring him to disagree. Surely someone will come to my aid.

SOX

I. M. Pei, a Chinese American architect, died at the age of 102. Venerable and gracious, his controversial glass pyramid standing at the entrance to the Louvre in Paris is a singular mark of his creative genius. Born in the Chinese city of Guangzhou and raised in Hong Kong and Shanghai, he drew inspiration from the gardens of Suzhou, particularly the delightfully named Humble Administrator's Garden, which was first laid out in 1509 AD.

I worked for six years on a campus that heralded the iconic works of architects Richard Neutra and Philip Johnson, and was privileged to work closely with Richard Meier as he completed his work on the Getty Center in Los Angeles and then designed a building for our campus. In and out of the Getty Center with him, wearing a hardhat, and visiting other of his completed works, I learned a lot.

Now married to Mr. T, an architect, I sometimes introduce him by saying that he was an architect. Although retired for many years, he bristles and declares, "I *still am* an architect!" and I quietly smack my hand.

I was in Richmond last week, schlepping, listening to the tired feet on pavements, trekking on from one daily adventure to another, when I found myself near the Coles supermarket. As I schlepped past the fruit and vegetables doggedly blocking my way into the store, I walked past a tall gentleman, and a flash of birdlike brightness caught my eye. It was wintery cold out there in Richmond, yet he was wearing shorts and sandals, making the toes of his socks easy to spy. Perhaps he wanted a passerby to be as pleased with his sock toes as he was. Perhaps they made him smile. These were toes of joy. One sock was bright red, the other bright blue.

These were sock toes that needed to wriggle, or be photographed, or dance, or do the Highland fling, or be used to point, or to simply stand by the vegetable counter inside the Coles supermarket and wait for me.

They made me smile. I believe they would have made I. M. Pei smile too. I was inspired.

MORE SOX

It all began with Jordie, who came to stay for the weekend, all burdened about with three, large, soft-pink, carry bags of girlie goodies. Since Jordie was only coming to stay for one night, it was going to be quite a revelation to see what she deemed important enough to pack and load onto her thin, little, six-year-old shoulders.

Much planning had gone into what we might do to keep Jordie and her eight-year-old brother Sammie occupied for the weekend. Our apartment is spacious but has no backyard in which to deposit overactive children so that they might run off a little steam. And steam they had, in abundance. We made flags to wave at the football. We made cards that they filled with loving greetings to take home to their parents. At least Jordie made cards filled with loving greetings to take home to her parents. Sammie was more inclined to drawings of Evel Knievel or Darth Vader, skulls and cross bones, guns and swords. Jordie had learned early which side her bread was buttered on. Give a little sugar away and all kinds of good things will follow. A few love hearts and kisses on paper were rewarded with a cuddle or two and a kiss or two and lots of loving verbal praise, including such things as what a sweet, good, kind, and loving girl she was. And, "Look everyone, see what Jordie has done."

Jordie does not so much move in competition with her boy cousins, so as to move into an imperious and untouchable stance when they are in town. I observed her at the tender age of two, in the midst of a gathering of the clan, bedlam being alive at the adult's knee-height as the boy cousins cavorted with total disregard for decorum. Jordie moved through their competitive play with a commanding wave of her tiny hand, and was heard to say in a loud and unmistakably determined voice, "Get out of my way!" They did.

So there she was on our doorstep, all burdened down with three pink bags and their important contents. The little mouth opened to reveal that wonder of life, wobbly teeth. All gaps were duly inspected, while the most wobbly of all was twisted and turned, bent back until it all but disappeared, poked with the tongue and various sticky little fingers until it appeared to be begging for mercy. But the wobbly tooth stayed right where it was, while Jordie chatted at such a rate that it was a near impossibility to follow her from one topic to another, hands flapping, teeth wobbling, lips grinning, and laughter bubbling from her like a life-giving spring.

The three pink bags eventually made their way out of the car, through the front gate, through the glass door, into the elevator and out, into our apartment, and down the hallway to her bedroom. There, they were deposited with much huffing and puffing, gasping and dramatic carryings-on. And from there, we were entertained with the revelation of their contents, a dribble at a time over the next two days.

It took but a few minutes for our apartment to be strewn with the delights of Jordie and Sammie's creative efforts as a result of them having been endowed with plastic boxes full to the brim with scraps of ribbon in bright colors, cardboard pieces, scissors, marking pens, glue sticks, leftover beads, and other bits and bobs all designed to seduce two young children into a moment or two of quiet activity.

Now, I love clothes, and I do not know if it possible to inherit such a characteristic, but it is certainly a characteristic Jordie and I share. Out came for the inspection and admiration of all, a pair of black tights. But not just any old black tights. First of all, they were tiny. They fitted over her cute little bottom to perfection. But the sides! Oh, the sides. We had to pay close and adoring attention. All had to gather at the showing, for there from toe to hip, were the spangliest spangles a girl could ever dream of. Much pirouetting and twirling and we were ready for the next. Boots. But not just any old boots. Not practical rubber boots. These were the Parisian kind of boots, all grey suede with furry turnovers at the knee. Plus a few spangles. The tiny feet clad in the spangly tights went straight into the grey suede and fur-trimmed boots, and the lot was topped off with a sweater made of shiny black material. But we were not done. There were two more pairs of boots, the very best being saved until last. These, evidently the pièce-de-resistance, were bright fluorescent pink. With spangles. Of course. These boots were perfect for twirling in the particular way known only to girls. Then they were used for a little strutting of the type usually seen by models on the catwalks of New York. A few dance steps, followed by a little march back to the bedroom to explore for more treasures with which to show off.

And then there was the hair. Jordie is the kind of girl who loves her hair. She loves it so much that she declared when she arrived for this much-anticipated visit, that she had not brushed it for a week! The level of surprise I felt must have shown on my face, for Jordie hastened to explain that she likes her curly hair, and if she does not brush it, it becomes much curlier. The truth is that it took a great deal of grandmotherly love to encourage the washing and conditioning, then detangling and fluffing up of said hair. Fluffing up is in fact a lot of what Jordie loves to do. It reminds me of my Auntie Dell. I never saw Auntie Dell do a day's work, but she was extremely good at fluffing up, always arriving in a cloud of matronly perfume, fur collars, corsages of violets, high heels, and lipstick. The thing is, though; Jordie never did meet Auntie Dell. Could it be a genetic characteristic?

By the time two days marched to a close, and Jordie's parents arrived to take her in tow, Jordie was ready to leave us buried ever so gently in a swirl of paper covered with love hearts and birds, flowers and trees, and yellow suns always placed *just* so in the corner of the art piece. I remember drawing suns just so in the corners of my artwork when I was a child. Where could that idea come from? I never did see the sun in the corner of anything, and neither did Jordie. The swirl was followed by streamers of enough colors to compete with Joseph's coat, a veritable plethora of color—streamers that she had draped with the help of Mr. T from one end of the bookcase to the other, over lamps, across the television to finally dip onto the floor in exhaustion. Embroiled in this commotion of love were dozens of balloons, in various stages of blown-upness. Red and blue, green and yellow. Blobs of light and joy.

Clothes had been repacked into their pink bags. Jackets, tops, hair bands, tights with spangles, boots, worn and not worn, pink slippers, pink dressing gown. Such accoutrements were all for a little darling who springs into our presence with the light of life in her eyes. The pink sleeping bag was stuffed right back into its little pink sack, tight as a butterfly into its chrysalis. She left us with cards full of her exuberant love, including one which said, "Dear Papa and Gigi, I love you so much I want to hug you for a long time."

She will go a long way, that girl.

As the last remnants were cleared away, the dishes washed, the tables wiped, the popped and deflated balloons tossed, and photographs downloaded onto the computer—there it was, one last loving little reminder of the light and joy an effervescent child can bring. One sock. It was only a little sock. In fact, it was a very little sock. Jordie is a very little girl. Just one lonely little navy-blue sock, left behind with its partner off to some other part of the planet. Navy blue—I thought—doesn't look like our Miss Spangles Unlimited Jordie. But it was hers. No one else in the whereabouts could fit into it. It was like Cinderella's lost slipper, waiting for the right-sized foot to slip right on in. It was a little symbol, a lovely little dot on the horizon of our life, a left-behind sock, a memory of a small ray of sunshine who came and went in a blaze of love and femininity, all fluffed up with love and the accoutrements of a little girl's life.

ON A CLOUD

My immediate plan was to get off the tram at Elizabeth Street and head for the Myer Department store. I was in a lather of frustration as I schlepped through the city crowds, swearing away to myself. "What a jolly waste of time this all is," I thought. "What a great big nuisance!"

The "stuff" I was lugging had been delivered to our door. That was the easy part. Returning it all was much harder. But hardest of all had been shoving its whole self back inside the packaging so that it looked as though I had neither opened nor touched it. "It was all that lady's fault too!" I fumed to myself. She who had inspired me to purchase a jumbuck, summer-weight, feather-light doona.

Many months prior I had had a friendly chat with her, over a jumbuck wool mattress protector I purchased. I had learned that she was Greek, that her husband had been very ill, and that they had had to postpone a longed-for vacation in Greece last year as a result. He was well enough now, she told me, so that they were off to Greece this year. They could not take out travel insurance any more, but they were determined to go despite that.

We bonded over husband, illness, travel, canceled travel, lack of insurance, land "going now anyway." As we were farewelling each other like a couple of old friends, she mentioned that she herself had purchased the same jumbuck wool mattress protector that I had just purchased from her. She loved it. So did her husband.

"But, did I know ...?" And she went on to tell me about a feather-weight, feather-light doona for summer that she had purchased and that she and her husband both loved. "It's just like sleeping under a cloud," she told me, smiling with pleasure at the thought.

In the six months since, her words, "Like sleeping under a cloud", had been in my mouth, tasting like fairy floss—until I went back the Myer department store and bought one. But unlike the good lady's husband, Mr. T did not like it, and neither did Mr. T want to keep it. Hence the tram and me lugging a big blue plastic Ikea bag with its feather-weight, feather-light contents slipping and sliding around my legs like flotsam and jetsam as I endeavored to maneuver it on and off the tram and through the barrage of traffic and oncoming pedestrians. I was hoping to get to Myer, return the darned thing and be back to Flinders Lane for a writing class by 11:00 a.m.

She was gracious and understanding about my return. But as I walked away, I heard myself saying to myself, "I think a cotton one would have been better." And I smack my hand over my mouth mentally at the thought. I smack my hand too. "Don't," I tell myself.

Mr. T and I traveled together into previously unexplored
parts of the paper bag of life.

THE TRIP OF A LIFETIME

Mr. T's birthday was to be celebrated in Machu Picchu, until a dramatic volcano erupted in Chile, resulting in the Los Angeles airport being closed—and scramble and panic worldwide. I kept a small radio plugged into my ear all night, yet only once in that night was the specter of the volcanic hell in Chile spoken of.

We were squeezed onto a Melbourne to Sydney flight only one day later, to overnight in Sydney and then fly direct to Santiago, Chile, bypassing Buenos Aires. Much choofing of that untimely volcano could be seen on our computer screens as we held our corporate breath, waiting to see what the day might bring. Neither of us slept much, we were flattened emotionally but holding onto a thread of hope that our much-anticipated tour of the Inca Empire would not be aborted.

The hotel bus coordinator counted our orange boarding cards ferociously and repeatedly until he was satisfied that all were accounted for. The Qantas lounge was light-filled and half empty, and once aboard LAN Chilean Airlines, we were bathed in luxury, and I felt the bliss. With Bose headphones plugged in, we began to recover from the stress of the canceled flight, while I reminded myself that volcanoes can interfere with the best laid plans. They seemed to follow us. An Icelandic volcano had caused us canceled flights in the prior year, and now this Chilean eruption has disrupted our plans as well. I tried to relax and allow the gentle Spanish words that enveloped us to wrap harmonics around my soul as I reflected on Machu Picchu, which had been crisscrossed through the ages with competing empires: Spanish, French, Prussian, Inca—and most recently, Chilean and dictatorial.

In Santiago we were besotted with the fizzed lemon drinks which reminded me of Italian Limoncello, succumbed to coffee they called Venetian but we would call cappuccino, Americano coffee that we would call long black, and a wine whose name we did not know but which was whisked to our table after an exchange that went like this: "Wine?" "Wine? Yes please!" This with much nodding of my head. Two fingers were lifted and two eyebrows raised and Presto! Wine arrived. Over our nameless wine we had a lengthy discussion about family life, and I shed a few tears as our conclusion was that the only way we could keep in touch with our particular tribal diaspora was to move into a regulated time for Skype, and I hoped fervently that there would be less anxiety re the volcano's effect on tomorrow's travel.

Showered and packed the next morning, I realized that I had left my favorite hand-spun and hand-woven alpaca scarf on the chair at Poco Loco Restaurant on Avenue Basque Norte the night before. A walk there after breakfast only resulted in my looking mournfully in the window at crumb-covered tables. No amount of knocking woke even the dead. I was hoping for the odd cook or even a potato peeler who could offer assistance, and was mad at myself and sad at the loss. I would rather have given it away.

I looked out over the Pacific coast of Peru, which seemed exotic and mysterious, but I could find no link to all the study of British and Modern History I had done. I needed much listening and looking and learning. A throwaway line from a young Chilean gentleman yesterday, "Francis Drake was a pirate too," left me short of the words for which I am famously long. Was he?

Found the scarf. At the restaurant.

A breakfast gathering was held the next day in a pavilion adjoining the hotel, where nametags were handed out at a meet-and-greet with Ronnie, our Costa Rican tour guide. Over beautifully served food we met Diane and John from California who had been married just one year, she sporting a broken nose from a fall. Diane had been raised in Holland, Michigan and was more than surprised to find that I had been there, and to Zeeland, Michigan. More Dutch than the Dutch they were, in that part of the US. Diane had been a missionary in Mexico City for twenty years, and John's first wife had died from cancer.

We toured a monastery built in the 1500s, a church built in the 1600s, and a new museum brimming with Inca and pre-Inca artifacts. Then lunch was held in a private Spanish home that reminded me of Santa Barbara. The contessa was of the sixteenth generation to reside there. We ate dinner in an architect's home, where thousands of nativities were on display.

The hardiest folk set off at 6:00 a.m. the next day to see

the Nazca Lines, a group of pre-Columbian geoglyphs etched into the desert sand. We were glad we opted out when they returned after a sixteen-hour day with very mixed responses. We had chosen to visit an art museum, a venue made up of a group of three small pavilions in a Victorian exhibition center and surrounded by parks. There, the young people manning the gallery seemed unprepared for us, as some were fixing the computer at the front desk, some were opening doors, and some were switching on lights as our sweet little Peruvian guide spoke with loving pride of, "the beautiful Peruvian this," or the "beautiful Peruvian that." Fine contemporary Peruvian art from the 1950s was on display.

But outside, it was an observably poor country; narrow houses, built cheek by jowl, had no gardens and only a small car space fenced off in front of each house. "The beautiful flowers," our guide referred to were large cacti flourishing in pots. Much street sweeping was in progress by enthusiastic individuals who deftly manhandled one leaf at a time.

FEELIN' FAR TOO SMUG

We were almost completely packed a week early. Mr. T said we could have left then. I thought not, but then who am I to say what I think. It turned out that *not* was what it was. That last week before takeoff was a week of dashing and darting from one triviality to another. "Details unlimited" became my second name. Details of sixteen flights and seventy folk to contact all kept me at the computer for more time than any girl would enjoy. In between all that, there were three meals a day to think about, shop for, and prepare—washing to be done, ironing to be done, plant watering and cat brushing to be done, along with floor vacuuming and dusting—and the oven to be cleaned and ready for our return.

The night before the big getaway Gerry had come up from his apartment below to get the gen on plant watering while we were away. I was in the mood for a ten-minute courtesy call, but Gerry's ideas were different when he knocked on our door. He was ready for a wind down. "No food," he said in answer to my offer. "No thank you. No cheese and crackers, no nuts—just red wine, thank you." Three glasses of red wine later and Gerry was decidedly congenial and comfortably settled in, while I was feeling decidedly uncongenial and uncomfortable. When I left him with Mr. T and went to get on with my work, he was still telling stories of his own brilliance and of his ability to quaff alcohol.

Mr. T and I hailed our taxi the next morning and were on our way to the airport when I realized I had left my prescription sunglasses behind, still in their smart little case and resting on the round wooden table where I had placed them carefully the night before so that I would not possibly forget them. Frustration.

At the airport we rallied our strength to proceed through what seemed to be the total population of Australia and Asia combined, gathered for the sole purpose of blocking our way to the Qantas counter.

The temperature was mooted to reach 34 degrees Celsius

and the day was already warming up. And I? I was warming up too. I was wearing a fur coat. I needed fur to survive the cold winter in Sweden where we were headed after California. Lugging so much luggage, carrying the fur coat was more than I could manage, so I wore it and was melting inside.

Slowly, we trundled our baggage through the madding crowd towards the check-in. A serious drama with the baggage conveyer-belt system led to much standing on one foot and then the other, as well as much huffing and puffing, until we were through to Customs and to the final security check of carry-on baggage.

And then? Mr. T could not really have packed scissors in his carry-on— could he? He could. And he did. I was incredulous, but the scissors just glared at us, as did the Customs officer. They were my hairdressing scissors and seriously expensive. I was not prepared to throw them in the bin. A few helpful words of advice from Qantas and Mr. T raced off back through the total population of Australia and Asia in order to purchase a padded bag. He would then mail the unhappy scissors back home where they belonged. Trouble raised its head one more time. In his haste, Mr. T had forgotten his wallet. Back through the madding crowds he raced to me, busy filling out Customs forms. More incredulity from me and once more he was off, wallet in hand. He returned sweaty and panicked. The scissors were on their way and it was almost time for boarding.

Except that it wasn't. Conveyer-belt troubles had now delayed the flight for one more hour. We wended our way through more trailing queues and finally up the wrong escalator. Down another escalator we rode and up the right one until we found respite in the lounge, where we flopped into our seats more than ready for a stiff drink, despite the fact that it was only 9:00 a.m. By the time we had finished Bircher muesli and fruit, and downed a coffee or two, we started to settle and sanitize.

As we stood to head for our flight, I spied a cheap pair of sunglasses a passenger had left in their haste. They were on a seat close by, and as there was not a person in sight, I swiped them into my bag with only the smallest twinge of guilt. Now I would be able to drive on the California freeways without squinting and would not suffer from snow blindness in Sweden. Leaving behind my multi-focal, light sensitive, huge, everywhere, every-day, every purpose sunglasses was a bad miss.

Seated on board our plane at last, we were too relieved to talk, and wafted into a haze of business class mist.

SLEEPLESS IN DOHA

It bleated all night. Repeatedly. Shriekingly loud and urgent. Lives were at stake. Many lives. Our lives. "Notice me! Notice me!"—it cried with each repeat.

Hamad International Airport in Doha, Qatar, is a wondrous, award-winning place. Lofty ceilings offer protective cover to even the meekest. With its calm and quiet elegance, it is attuned to the needs of travelers crisscrossing the world.

Even the name *Doha* evokes a sense of place—the air is abuzz with enticing stories, oil, wealth, and the exotic.

I had spied and photographed an Arab in his magnificent *thwab*, *keffiyeh*, and *agal* striding proudly through the airport, a falcon perched on his arm. Two more gentlemen, similarly attired and also sporting perching falcons, followed in his train, a magnificent parade for my absolute pleasure. The flight that had taken us from Melbourne to Doha, and then on to Copenhagen, had been a calm and pleasant experience.

The pickup at Copenhagen Airport was on time, and the Tivoli Hotel was perfect for a two-day precruise stay. We had plans to explore the loveliness of the city. But everything in the world was changing so rapidly that by the time we turned on our television, news of the rogue virus COVID-19 was bursting through the screen, unrelenting. We did manage a forty-minute walk along the canal-front and into the center of town through a hurricane—although "I am not sure I would go out there," worried the front desk manager. But as hardy Australians who needed a bit of fresh air after many hours of flying, we smiled and went on our way. Copenhagen was quiet.

Back inside the Tivoli Hotel, the television set beckoned us to perch on our bed yet again. In the time we had been out walking, news had moved from serious to urgent. People were sickening all over the world. All commentators sounded grim. All looked grim. People were dying. Especially in Europe. In Europe? Wasn't that where we were? We had left Australia with noses pointed towards Copenhagen with plans for a short flight to Bergen, where we would board the Hutigruten ship, MS *Trollfjord*, for a twelve-day cruise though the waters of the North Sea to Kirkenes and back.

The MS *Trollfjord* was named after the spectacular Trollfjord in Lofoten. I felt a connection to Lofoten because my nephew's beautiful wife, Hilde, had come to the US from there as a four-year-old, and her family visited their property in the Lofoten Islands annually. The last time we took a Hutigruten cruise on these same waters, our Swedish in-laws, Lars and Gunbritt, joined us on board after a hiking holiday in the Lofoten Islands. I was moving dizzyingly fast into a world full of Nordic rellies.

We had been scheduled to visit Floro, Molde, Kristiansund, Rorvik, Trondheim, Bronnoysund, Svolvaer, Stokmarknes, Skjervoy, Oksfjord, Berlevag and Batsfjord as we sailed north to Kirkenes, and then to sail back south to Bergen. It all sounded so cold and so Norwegian and so promising. The travel agent had guaranteed a view of the Northern Lights, and if we did not see the lights, a free trip. That by itself was enough to get Mr. T's Scottish blood racing. With that offer and the chance to visit our Swedish clan in Gothenburg on the way home, we were on the trip of a lifetime. We thought. As much as I had wished to see the Northern Lights for decades, I had been puzzled that such a spectacular promise could be made and joked that some nefarious person would run up onto the deck near midnight waving a torch, then run off to hide. A minute or two later an announcement in Norwegian would alert us to the fact that they were sorry for all those who had missed the light show.

But now I was far from joking. Somewhere in a quiet place,

that feisty little killer COVID-19 had evolved and given birth to myriads of babies. Clinging stealthily to the fabric of many lives, it had attached and reattached millions of times while we were sitting on our bed in Copenhagen's Tivoli Hotel trying not to panic. We sucked in our breath, glanced at each other—horrified, turned back to the news of the Grim Reaper on television, and grimaced at the impossibility of our situation. Before we had left Australia, serious news about the minute killer had caused us to be thoughtful, so we had asked three doctors for their advice. Each had said, "Go. You could just as well catch it here as there." We did go. We went. We had gone. We were here. And nothing would ever be the same.

At the front desk of the Tivoli Hotel, Assad's inquiries left him looking studiedly serious when he put down the phone. The cruise had been canceled. Not one of the Australians in the hotel had been notified by the travel agent. As the rumble of trouble grew into a shout and then a roar, Toby and Linda graciously offered that we head for their Gothenburg home—*pronto*. There was suddenly much to do, all of it urgent.

Despite holding for hours on the phone, we were unable to speak with anyone at Qatar Airways or get a reply to our emails. I emailed the Consul General for Australia. I did not receive a reply. In desperation I even emailed Aqel Biltaji, the former mayor

Aqel Biltaji, former mayor of Aman.

of Amman, tourism adviser to King Abdullah II and chief of Aqaba's city council. I had looked after him twenty years before and had liked him well. I always remembered his graciousness and his lovely name. He had even invited me to visit. Would I have made such an impression on his busy mind that he remembered me? Apparently not. Perhaps he was occupied in a deep conversation with the King.

Assad's sober suggestion was that Mr. T and I take a cab for the airport immediately. Once there, we might be able to persuade Qatar Airways to change our flights. But they could not. "Only the travel agent can do that." We loped on to the SAS counter, suitcases complaining beside us. There we stood in line with a small quietly urgent group until, tickets in hand, we ran for a plane bound for Gothenburg, family, and home. That little metal tube of a plane was packed to the gills, bristling with the energy of bodies on high alert. In Gothenburg we discovered that Denmark had closed its borders ten minutes after we had flown out. No wonder Assad of the front desk had been so serious. The ratty little virus was on our tail. Back at the Tivoli in Copenhagen the few other Australians booked on the same trip sat quietly in the lobby, waiting for a bus that did not come. And never did come.

In Gothenburg we threaded our way through the curiosities of high drama outside and serenity inside. We held close in our hearts the precious weight of our family—Toby Benjamin, Linda Kristina, Ebba Kristina, and Oskar Benjamin Henry— who welcomed us and adjusted every part of their lives as the world roiled, as their jobs were threatened, and the children committed to speaking English to us and giving up their beds. There was no complaint. We were offered healthy feasts, quiet conversation, and simple adaption. We were nurtured by their love. But we could not hug. And we could not visit the in-laws, as the risk was too great. Ebba and I made up an "alternative to hugging" dance. We stood far apart, facing. We spread our arms wide and rotated slowly, one way and then the other. We grinned ruefully, and then did it again. I tried not to cry. I try not to cry as I write. Will we have the opportunity to see them again?

After three days and with precious memories of Gothenburg time in our pockets—along with videos of the new puppy, Chloe, who was oblivious to all viral threats—we prepared to leave. But life offered another moment of joy. Before we said goodbye, we were blessed by a visit from three deer, walking down out of the forest behind to forage near Toby's magnificent vegetable garden, then nimbly tripping back up the hill and disappearing into the greenery.

We flew back to Copenhagen—and the transit lounge where we remained sleepless all night. We had desired to hunker down for a sleep in the business class lounge. But that lounge closed at 9:30 p.m., so we were forced to wander into the transit lounge, despite the fact that our connecting flight was not due to fly out until 8:30 the next morning. We were not permitted to leave that transit lounge; if we did, we would be stuck—we did not know exactly where or for how long. Sleeping there was our only choice. By 10:00 p.m. it was almost entirely deserted except for a few other hardy souls who had found a spot to try for sleep. We found a spot too. And we tried for sleep.

It bleated all night. Repeatedly. Shriekingly loud and urgent. Lives were at stake. Many lives. Our lives. "Notice me! Notice me!"—it cried with each repeat. All night, the bleating assailed us, repeatedly, first in English, then in Danish.

Danish? I thought we were in Doha. My befuddled mind had settled me down in a hallway in the transit lounge in Doha. But no, we had not traveled that far yet. We had flown only the first leg home—from the family in Gothenburg to Copenhagen— and emerged safe into the arms of the Copenhagen airport. Our cruise was canceled, our trip aborted, and this transit lounge was where we must make our nest for the night. That night Denmark was also a country appropriately determined that every person within a ten-mile radius of the airport be fully informed about distancing, hand washing, and sanitiz- ing—and why it was all so important. After the dramas of the past few days we did understand their imperative, but we also desired sleep, which was beyond us. We were not sleepless in Doha. Instead we were sitting up, wearily trying for grace in a difficult time in the welcoming and practical arms of Copenhagen Airport. We were sleepless in Copenhagen.

Someone had placed light blankets here and there on the seating with loving care. But I could only look askance, not knowing who else may have made use of them, leaving a tiny killer or two lurking in their folds, grinning mercilessly. I loved the thoughtfulness of the gesture, but I did not love the thought of using the blankets. The only do-it-yourself coffee machine was out of order, blinking its red eye at me to find a member of staff to help. There being no member of staff in sight, I wandered sleepily from one end of the transit lounge to the other. A cleaner or two appeared as the night wore on, vacuum cleaner trailing. By five-thirty in the morning, when the business class lounge reopened, we were grovelingly grateful to find fresh food and enough long couches for us to rest on for the hours we still had prior to takeoff, that is, takeoff for Doha and the Hamad International Airport.

Our flight from Copenhagen to Doha on Qatar Airways offered us the amusement of being the only two folk in business class. It even tickled the fancy of the crew, who came to us and chatted, sharing stories. One man's son was stuck in Peru with a group of young friends. The stunningly beautiful stewardess Z told me that if she returned to her family in Qatar, she could not leave again and therefore could not work. And so she flies from one side of the world to the other, dodging COVID-19 while she tries to decide what she will do. Back at the Tivoli Hotel in Copenhagen, staff had been deciding in what order they would take their unpaid leave in an effort to keep their jobs. Their restaurants were closing. Where would guests eat?

The terminal in Doha was as elegant and unruffled as I had remembered. The food was elegant and unruffled too, as were the staff. But all travelers were somberly uncommunicative, holding their corporate breath as they hoped for an escape into the air. By the time we landed in Melbourne we felt as though we had eaten a huge meal and were full. But this meal had not satisfied.

Mr. T's daughter, Natasha, who had kept closely in touch, came to the airport with her daughter Emily so that they could bring two cars, our car as well as theirs. Their concern was that we should not take a taxi, a Uber, or a bus—and it was certainly too far for us to consider walking to Richmond dragging our luggage. They welcomed us, waved us off to our car, and moved quickly away from our orbit. We stashed both suitcases and relief into the car's trunk.

At home, The Silos was undisturbed by any notion of the unfolding drama of COVID-19. The refrigerator was stocked with nourishing food—and love.

The city sparkled at night. The sun rose and set, keeping its own rhythm. The magpies gurgled their joy from the balcony. Neighbors offered food and assistance.

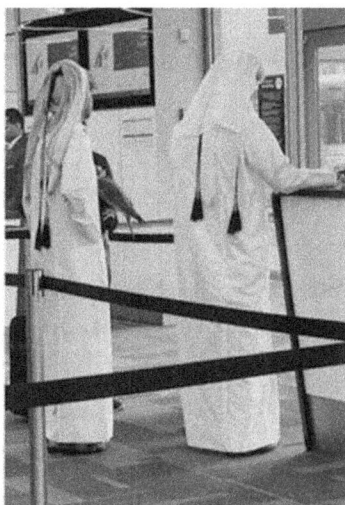

Seen in Hamad International Airport

But now? We were sleepless in Richmond.

Some of our journeys together were pain ravaged,
as they can be.

PEACE AT ANY PRICE

Mr. T had a harrowing year as he withstood the grim challenge of an aggressive and chaotic skin cancer. Each grueling surgery was followed by a pathology report. Each report stated that "the margins were clear." But it was a lie. Who or what lied, it is impossible for me to say. But the result was that the attending physician had to come in, cap in hand, to explain the unexplainable. The cancer had skipped the clear margins and was at its gruesome work again.

I was reflecting on all this as I trundled towards Richmond on the tram, following some splendid time with Maggie. Maggie loves Melbourne. Maggie also knows a lot about Melbourne. Maggie *knows places*. I am a perfectly willing follower as she turns Melbourne corners, climbs Melbourne stairways known only to her, points out history with every second step, dives into basements, and generally affords me much pleasure. Today we took a tour of the Town Hall. It was enlightening in many ways. We then ate at a small restaurant overlooking Collins Street, feeling private and hoping that no one else would ever find this place.

Following that, we trammed our way to King Street, where we enjoyed Campari and gossip in a rooftop bar, chuffed older ladies amongst a group of middle-aged businessmen doing middle-aged businessman things over a drink or two.

LIFE IN A PAPER BAG

Sitting on the tram after all that adventure and reflecting on the last medical-filled year for Mr. T, I opened my trusty iPhone and joined all the other tram-travelers in reading some of my emails.

Friend Elizabeth suggested a Thai restaurant in Collingwood for our next book club meeting, as our preferred venue was no longer to be open on Monday nights. I sent that information to other members. We meet only once a month and have not discussed a book seriously for many moons, but do very much enjoy our little outing and each other's company.

Still on the tram and still with my trusty iPhone in hand, I read further that Sir Richard Branson owns a rather interesting resort island in the vicinity of Noosa Heads, Queensland, and is advertising it as a possible rental for those in need of a little break. A SANCTUARY OF SECLUSION, it said. YOUR PRIVATE ISLAND ESCAPE, it said further. Being partial to warm weather and also being partial to any luxury that could be offered, and also thinking of a suitable gift for the beleaguered Mr. T for his upcoming birthday, I went into full gear and looked up said resort island.

Makepeace Island it is called. Good name. The accompanying blurb caused it to sound as though it was just what we needed. Your private island escape, a sanctuary of seclusion, and a place to escape and unwind. What more could I offer Mr. T? I clicked suitable dates for us into their calendar to coincide with Mr. T's birthday. Eight days should suffice. I was still trundling along on the tram towards Richmond and beginning to fill with excited anticipation, when hey presto, there it was: a response from Makepeace Island. So soon!

ALL INCLUSIVE, and, IN HIGH DEMAND, my screen cried out with joy. WE HAVE ONE ROOM LEFT, it said. BREAKFAST INCLUDED, it said. SENSITIVELY DEVELOPED IN KEEPING WITH THE COASTAL WILDERNESS, it said further. LUXURIOUS EXCLUSIVITY, it said. MODERN CONTEMPORARY LIVING COMBINED WITH TRADITIONAL TROPICAL-ISLAND DESIGN THAT IS IN COMPLETE HARMONY WITH NATURE, it said.

LAST MINUTE.COM.AU RATE, it said. SELECT YOUR ROOM. I could not easily understand how I could select our room if there was only one left. But there it all was. Wonderful. Breathtaking in fact. I was feeling refreshed just thinking about it. Mr. T could have all that tropical healing balm wash over him. I sat with my finger pointed, ready to click us right into Branson Heaven. Makepeace Island.

But wait—$41,360 AUD for eight nights?

I clicked again, and again, and even again, but that was all I could get my trusty iPhone to offer. But fear not, help was at hand. The angels of iPhone-land were there to aid and abet. Immediately below Branson Heaven, inscribed in golden illuminated letters, glowing pleadingly at me through the cell phone screen I read:

NOOSA CARAVAN PARK—4.3 STARS. FABULOUS! it said, (from 140 reviews). FREE CANCELLATION, it offered. PET FRIENDLY, it said. (Too bad our cat is dead.)

But one reviewer complained loudly that, "Seventy dollars for one night just because we came with two cars is overpriced."

On the other hand, many others said it was clean and spacious.

No free breakfast here though.

Too bad.

PROGNOSIS

He trod
through the green forest
of his life,
darkening now
with fear.

Reverently held high,
his future
was in manly hands.
But he owned it not.

Stark with brilliance,
the hallowed void of death
had replaced
his ownership of life,
by stealth.

Then she smiled
at him,
sweetly.

"I have your back,"
she said.

An arc of light,
as ancient as the mystery
of the stars
shot him through.

He trod on,
holding hope.

Willis saved the paper bags from his homemade sandwiches
until they were no longer able to be reused.

RECYCLING

I have wasted too much energy.
I am feeling tired.
I recognize more poignantly
the need to conserve.
Plastic.
Paper.
Money.
Time.
And energy.
I have always been a "give it away but don't waste it" kind of
person.
Now I see

that I have given far too much.
Energy, I mean.
Emotional.
Physical.
Mental.
Psychological.

It has taken me the sum of all my days to know of this.
"Be careful!" I admonish myself.
Grandchildren
are hardly tolerant
as I ask for a little help
with the computer.
And yet ...
while they can patronize with their kindness,
so can I,
with my wisdom.

To honor my days,
I endeavor to distill
that which is essential,
and offer it one sentence at a time,
at the gateway of their adult lives.
There sat the wise men,
at the gate of the city,
watching,
listening,
learning,

and offering wisdom.

"He who has an ear let him hear."

I am endeavoring to listen more.

And to offer wisdom with love.

Time is short.

WHICH BIN?

Trash night, and a major effort for me is to gather my energy, take myself outside, open the side gate, kick the monstrous trash bin onto its wheels, and roll it outside ready for the contents to be removed from my property the next day. For three years I have sifted and sorted my trash, so that each piece goes into the appropriate bin. For three years, every Tuesday night, I have kicked the bins up onto their wheels and dragged them outside.

Last Tuesday night I went out with my bins, to discover that all of the garden clippings which I had chopped and carried and dropped into the green bin with great care for recycling, were in fact in the wrong bin. To my horror I discovered that green clippings do not go into the green bin. Green clippings go into the brown bin. I had been logical, but I had not read the instructions. I should have read the big notice on the brown bin that said: Recycle. So there I stood, three bins full of my carefully sorted trash, all in the wrong bins.

How could I have done this? I mustered my courage and tried emptying all the bins, then swapping and sorting from one bin to another. I was grateful that there was no one in sight to laugh at my plight. The inside of a trash bin is not the most exciting place to spend a Tuesday night.

Eventually I gave up and tossed it all into one messy, stinky, unsorted mess. There has to be a lesson here somewhere. Choose your bins with care.

Sometimes I am more annoyed than I can manage to contain, as I pop my head out of my paper bag and observe life.

POETRY READING

She twirped on and on, and all I could think from the beginning to the end of the whole long carrying-on was, "Get a grip. Get a grip, girl. You think life has been tough because you had a passionate love affair when you were four years old. Get a grip." My mind raced as she read, sometimes ahead of her, sometimes with her, sometimes off to the side of her, but racing, racing all the time. I stamped my foot inwardly and wanted to yell loudly, "Get a grip."

She just seemed so very wrapped up in her own pain. She raved on and on about her remembered pain because she had loved her beautiful, god-like cousin when she was four years old. She loved him passionately. She was mesmerized. But he did not see her. He did not acknowledge her. He had had other things on his mind. As she melted down into the labor of her reading, she wiped her eyes, removing her glasses tenderly to do so in obeisance to the long-lost love. Her blue eyes glittered with unshed tears. She needed to stop and compose her ample self from time to time. But her mind was bedazzled still with the memory of him, her thoughts unrestrained. She was beset with the longing of a four-year-old.

In what manner she had carried on in this besotted state for so many years I cannot imagine, but the passion with which she expressed it as she read out her poem of longing and loss and guilt and shame, brought tears to her eyes, gulps of breath, and beads of sweat to her brow. She referred to Greek tragedy, and linked herself to the tragedies of the gods. She wailed and groaned, but I could only feel compassion for the poor man she had eventually married. How had he dealt with this other lover, so vividly alive in her imagination?

I sat, puffing with the energy I expended keeping that anger down within as the rest of the group groaned in pain with her, nodding and almost weeping at the tragedy of it all. They cajoled her into more and more of the same story until I thought I might scream if I do not remove myself from the room.

My son had a heart attack when he was nine months old. Should I write about that? Should I scarify my heart one more time with the knowledge that he died in my arms when he was four? He was my firstborn. Is that enough to get you to sit up and look out and over the high edge of your self-centered world? Will that give you a semblance of compassion? Is this what I am supposed to write about? So many years of working on courage and hope, gratitude, and generosity of spirit. Should I set them aside for the cause of the written word?

I cannot bear the self-indulgence of it all. I could well be walking into the wrong world, this world of self-expression. I have a friend who had both breasts removed with cancer last year. She has a son who is more than forty years old. He is so mentally and physically handicapped that he can come home to her only on the weekends. She is now so unwell she cannot have him at home. She grieves for him. She has cared for him alone for the past thirty years. Her husband died of cancer. She has three other children. This is what I call pain. I have a friend whose husband left her with six children, the youngest two being twins. Is this enough pain? I have a friend whose husband left her two weeks before her first babe was born. He faked his own death, then reappeared without a word on the babe's first birthday. They say he came back for the family money. He left again after the next child was born. Is this enough pain? My first husband tried to kill me. I ran for my life. I lived in a barn for three months. Is this enough pain?

I will not go on. And I beg of you, "Please do not go on with your self-indulgent twaddle." Please, write another poem. Tell us your story, but do not labor us with the weight of your conflicted love. We all have conflicted loves. We all carry pain and grief and loss—some of us have far too much too bear. But the blue sky we see when we can get our heads up helps us to take one more breath of fresh air, or one more step, or produce one more shadow of a smile, or a tentative touch of love to a friend in need, or an understanding with a more compassionate heart of the way it might be for most of the rest of the world, suffering in ways that we cannot comprehend.

I need music and laughter. I, too, need to cry, but I need to compel myself to look at flowers opening, a bird flying past—or gain strength from a great tree to hug. I need the smile of a babe, the smell of a puppy, the antics of a kitten to help me bear my losses and those of my friends.

Your words are clever, but they weigh me down. I cannot keep listening to you. Please write another poem.

SURPRISED BY CONTENTMENT

Contentment has rarely moved over my life sweet and simple—although love, the sense of physical well-being, joy at sunset, unpolluted air, children's laughter, the companionship of good friends, a glass of good wine, a warm fire, or the challenge of a good book have occasionally brought it. I count the people who could acknowledge themselves to be truly content—and try to think of the last time I heard contentment discussed, or longed for, or experienced—and am startled by the lack.

A friend of mine, her own life marked by courage, confided to me that her widowed mother living in a retirement village had written and underlined carefully at the top of each page of her daily calendar, "I will be content," and I thought this to be heroic discipline.

There have been times when something precious has been taken away, or something cherished has gone from my life—a friend has died, a child has left home for the first time, a marriage looked forward to with hope has been abandoned—or when financial loss has been so enormous as to leave me without the capacity to think—times when the small and large losses join hands to overwhelm and rob me of contentment.

Is it possible that in desolation of spirit, contentment could come by choice? How courageous a choice, to give way to a commitment to be content, stepping towards a place not yet seen, a future not yet comprehended.

Surprises have been the given in my life, as it has ebbed and flowed. Can I be surprised by contentment, or by joy? Can I be surprised by the contentment that comes as a choice as well as that which comes as an offering or a gift? And after all that, do I have the courage to hold it with both hands? Tight?

BLOODY PALACE

Bloody indeed. Bloody with my blood too.

Unlike the Romans who marched so carelessly through cities demanding and posturing and killing and raping and blaming and being important in the way you can be important if you are in charge and no one but no one has the power to stop you being in charge because should they consider it, it would be *off with your head* or some other horror that we will not discuss here because, should we do so, we would want to shut shop, go home, jam our feet firmly into pink fluffy slippers, and let the world march right past our window—and we would give not a flick of an eyebrow or a raise of a patrician nostril to notice its onward march. Unlike all of those dramatic men of history, I was a girl from Melbourne town who had the temerity to believe that the commitment made to her for ten years employment in California meant what it said: ten years employment in California.

But one fine day in spring, after only six years I was told to go. Leave. Vamoose. "We can no longer afford to pay you 'under California law,' etc., etc., etc." Washed up on a California beach like a stranded whale I was, hardly able to breathe. Trying to keep a shred of dignity. Having been told I was a gift from God when I was invited and agreed to come, now suddenly God had disappeared from the mix and it was all about money. I had been told somewhere in my past that the two did not really mix so well. They certainly did not mix on that particular California afternoon. I was out on my pretty ear, and sympathy was not offered. Fix it yourself was all I could hear. No one will fix this but you. Too much blood if you complain. We cannot have blood on our floors here. We have an image to protect. We have a reputation. We have shiny windows and shiny walls. People admire our shiny architecturally designed windows and walls. We even have specialists who come often to wash our shiny windows and our shiny walls. No one should be allowed to see what happens in our basement, but the windows are always shiny and clean. Distracting, really.

Complain? Who would believe you? Blood splashed a little on your shoes? We did not get any on our shoes. How come blood is splashed on yours? So long as you keep your mouth shut, we will not get any blood on us. Keep your mouth shut. Be kind to us. We may not be kind to you, but you be kind to us. We need you to be kind to us. We need to keep our reputation. Your reputation is not very important to us. We will not reveal that we are going under financially. You will not reveal that we are going under financially. You know too much, have seen too much, have gained too much power, and we are afraid of you. You have to go now.

We do not want to abandon you. But we will abandon you. To whatever. We really do not want to hear about what happens to you. We really do not care. "You have been amazing. In fact, you have been the most amazing thing that has ever happened here. That is why I am firing you personally. I usually have other people do this for me. But I do admire you more than I can say. There is no one I admire more than I admire you. But you have to go now." A master in the art of dissembling.

There was blood on the floor, too, with the Son of God. They tried to fire him. He was abandoned, washed up on the beach of *save himself*. He left them to their own devices and did not fight, although it was his right to do so. His work spoke for itself. He saw through everything. He knew them, and they did not like it. They did not want to be known. It is too fearful a thing to be known.

OFFERING

For many years we had worked alongside each other as colleagues, part of a tightly knit crew of eccentric, edgy, and committed band of helpers. At Saint Gabriel's School we had learned a lot about turn taking, the foundation for human intercourse and true conversation, and for diplomacy and empathy. The ribbons of life's paths had led Ruth to the south coast of New South Wales, and I was returned to the sun-burned land of Australia. We were looking to catch up. But how?

"This is what I can offer," Ruth said after some back and forth. My spirit unfurled. No barriers here. No equivocation. No apology. No excuse. No false modesty. This was a deeply thoughtful utterance. "This is what I can offer. I would be willing to drive halfway up the coast towards Sydney."

I look at my hands now, holding them palm up, and remember, "This is what I can offer." I will trust you to trust me without explanation, without excuse, and without apology. I will give, and you will receive. And then it will be your turn. You will give, and I will receive.

I stood on my back-porch years ago with the rain beating down. I was close to tears as I watched the swill of mud that was supposed to be my driveway. "Lord," I said, "I would love a real driveway. Then I could be relaxed enough to be gracious and kind as I welcomed my guests."

"I want you to be gracious and kind anyway," came the reply.

I was rebuked and I knew it.

I have learned so much and yet I know so little.

*There is so much more to learn in this paper bag of life.
Who will come my way? What will come my way?
What courage will I muster up? How much will I be willing
to give, or to receive? I long for gentleness, lack of judgement,
grace, mercy, and a dose of laughter at every new opening
of this paper bag of my life.*

*I have been privileged to meet profound and thoughtful
people who have shared with me some of their longings, losses,
and accumulated wisdom as life has changed around them.
Laughter has been medicine for me. I love to be tickled by the
precious trivialities of life, which lighten the load and lift my
spirits. I continue to seek to be unafraid.*

ACKNOWLEDGMENTS

Mr. T sat loving and patient, encouraging me daily as I sifted and sorted details of my writing.

My sons Luke Benjamin and Toby John lifted me up in thoughtfully practical and loving ways.

Colin Rolfe, Paul Cohen and Dory Mayo of Epigraph Books and Monkfish Book Publishing Company have held my hand and guided me with wit and grace. Kira Rosner has encouraged me with her patient love.

Friends have laughed me through.

I acknowledge with gratitude all who have oiled the wheels and cheered me onwards and forwards, offering their gifts of guidance and love as we ducked and weaved our way around Covid.

And in gratitude for the precious memory of my beloved friend Rhonda Fleming of the honeyed voice. With generous-hearted love she laughed and cried with me and welcomed me into her life and her home. I am indebted to her for many years of intimate friendship. She was remarkable in every way.

www.ingramcontent.com/pod-product-compliance
Lightning Source LLC
Chambersburg PA
CBHW031949090426
42739CB00006B/126